*By popular demand, the second printing of the new and revised second edition of*

# GREAT LIVIN' in GRUBBY TIMES

## Book II
of a five book series containing the most advanced
outdoor know-how out there.

Dedicated to

Politicians, who put RIGOR into our government, and
bureaucrats, who complete their effort by adding---
                    MORTIS.

Acknowledgements: To all of my Green Beret brothers, who have dedicated their lives to masterful outdoor creativity. They've lived to improve, and gone far beyond what we ever knew before.

Moreover, to our great and gracious God, the Master Survivalist, who conquered even death. It is to Him that our country and currency are dedicated. From Him I've gotten the strength and wisdom that enables me to pull it off---amazingly---in the face of unbelievable odds.

PUBLISHERS CATALOGING IN PUBLICATION PCIP:
Paul, Don 1937---
    Great Livin' in Grubby Times, Everybody's
Outdoor Survival Guide, Book II./by Don Paul.  2nd Ed.
    Includes index.
    ISBN: 0-938263-09-9
    1. Survival, outdoors.  Craftsmanship, outdoors,
Guide-books. 3. Outdoor Sports. I. Title. II. Outdoor
Living.  III.  Choose 'n use outdoor firearms.
    PN 147.P3   1992       796.042
                        GV191.7.P38. 1992

ISBN:  0-938263-09-9
Path Finder Publications
1296 E. Gibson Rd E-301, Woodland, Calif.  95776

# INTRODUCING. . .
## OUTDOOR BOOKS by
## PATH FINDER PUBLICATIONS
### New method books for outdoors people.

To earn money as an entrepreneur, take a place in society, grow in any business, and suceed as a writer or publisher, you have to focus on one thing. You develop a philosophy of business and set worthwhile, achievable goals.

This is our philosophy of business: We can only accept money in exchange for the best possible book we can produce. Our goal: To be best and go beyond any other knowledge out there on the same subject, and then to explain, in simple, easy-to-understand detail, the new methods we've discovered. We just don't want to publish words; we want to supply the newest, most innovative information we can. So--- we use independent editors and electronic manuscript scrubbers to make our books easy and quick to read. Pictures and illustrations make us easy to understand. We're care about saving your time. Hopefully, that's what we did in this book.

Path Finder began over 10 years ago.    Path Finder began over 10 years ago. We first invented a way never to get lost in the woods without using a map; it's called, _The Green Beret's Compass Course, Never Get lost._   Over 25,000 copies are in print.

Next, we added to our book list and widened our distribution. We published:

> _Everybody's Outdoor Survival Guide_
> _Everybody's Knife Bible_
> _24 + Ways to Use Your Hammock in the Field._

We develop and write about all kinds of new ideas and outdoor methods. We're the innovative people who wrote about:

√A 30¢ two ounce wilderness bed for sleeping above ground.

√The modification for your hunting knife sheath which enables you to see the floor of a jungle at night.

√A new shooting system to give you super bullet placement, day or night.

√Life saving, simple procedures for self defense.

√Terrain analysis for saving energy as you travel on foot over rough country.

√A new cold-weather survival method to keep you alive anywhere.

√A guide to water purification for any survivalist.

√How to use animals to double your survive-ability.

√Wind reading for super long distance shooting.

√Green Beret team concepts applied to survival groups so you can enjoy the ultimate life-style outdoors.

All of our books have gone into multiple editions. Most major outdoor magazines have reviewed our books and our systems have been adopted by many outdoor organizations.

We plan to publish *AMMO FOREVER,* by Craig Huber, a simplified reloading guide for survivalists in Sept 92. That's because your government may not be able to take away your guns, but they could shut off ammunition sales as they did in the L.A. riots. (It's apparently their mentality; the National Guard didn't have any either.)

If you're troubled by crime, try our forthcoming: *SECURE FROM CRIME--NEVER A VICTIM* . This book by C. Huber. takes a hold card attitude towards crime and cirminals. Maybe you should, too.

Currently, we're writing *EVERYBODY'S KNIFE BIBLE (BOOK II)* featuring over a hundred new ways to use your knives. Publish date: late in 92.

## (See the order coupons in the back of this book.)

---

**This survival book is one you can't live without---because without this book, you may not live. . .** It contains solid methods for surviving and living well through hard times, plus other Green Beret habits and mannerisms.

# GREAT LIVIN' in GRUBBY TIMES
## written by Green Beret's
### Table of Contents

# What Makes
## These Books the BEST?

# Never Before ...

. . . has Green Beret technique and know-how been made public!

. . . has any author travelled all over the world to interview Green Berets and get the best!

. . . have so many photos and illustrations dropped outdoor knowledge in your lap!

## WE AT PATHFINDER . . .

. . . publish new and novel methods for real outdoorsmen. Since 1982, we have sold thousands of outdoor books containing systems and methods used by the best woodsmen in the United States.

# CHAPTER I

## CHOOSING A WEAPON
## FOR SURVIVAL

Outdoor survival is like driving the Los Angeles Freeways. The circus is a lot more fun if you carry a gun to the shooting gallery. The question is, "What's the best shooter?"

This is a second printing. Since I wrote the first edition, things have gotten worse. So, firearms have become a major consideration for a lot of people who don't want to become victims.

Don't run out and buy a gun. Read this, and then select a firearm based on the various attributes found in the chart we furnish. You can't really choose properly unless you ask and answer these questions:

1. Who are you as far as shooting ability goes?
2. What does survival mean to you?
3. In what kind of surroundings will you survive?

"Know thyself," is a big key. For any firearm, the most important factor is the· nut behind the buttplate. You and your ability are the prime consideration. Are you bothered by recoil and noise?

Buying a firearm is like marrying a wife. Afterwards, how well you adjust to each other determines how well you face the world together and stay on target.

If you can't adjust to each other, the two of you aren't going anywhere. I weigh over 200 lbs, and even with years of shooting experience, I could never adjust to a .44 magnum's muzzle blast or recoil. I just had to get a divorce. The choice was simple. Either I had to admit I wasn't macho enough, or someday face a bear who would prove most painfully that, with this weapon, I couldn't hit the sky if I took careful aim on the moon.

Maybe you're smaller than average, not a trained gunner, and a little afraid. Don't despair. A light weight weapon will do just about everything that a heavyweight cannon will do---you just pull the trigger an extra time or two. Don't get caught up in a macho self image problem and buy a cannon. Be totally truthful about your own ability; that's the first step in marrying a weapon that will make you a real neighborhood influence.

2. How do YOU define survival?
A. Provide meat for food?
B. Protect crops and
livestock?
C. Protect home and family?
D. All of the above...?

My own choice is "D." It's important that you think about it for awhile, because your personal definition has a lot to do with how you apply the chart attributes. Most threats to home and family will come from short range, so you might not need a long range shooter. On the other hand, if you will be protecting crops and livestock, which are generally far from your home, you will need some long-distance influence, which means centerfire rifle.

Think about your surroundings. At what range will the average shot be taken? In Western Washington State, where I live, short ranges are common because brush and trees grow close together. In the Eastern desert, you sing the telephone song, and "reach out and touch someone." Weather is also important. Heavy rain? Scopes may fog, and blueing may rust. In frigid cold, I want hand operated actions, not automatics.

When you think about it, weapons have widely differing characteristics, qualities, or attributes, (seventeen of them) some of which are better for certain shooters, for a particular chore, or for a certain area of operation.

Once you have taken your own capabilities into account, defined survival for yourself and considered your surroundings, look at the WEAPONS ATTRIBUTE CHART. The applications of this chart will make the difference between buying a gun that goes boom to advertize your position, or a weapon that persuades people and animals to see things as you would like them to.

| | EFFECTIVE RANGE | SHOOTING / EASE OF MASTERY | LOADING / EASE OF MASTERY | RECOIL EASE | SILENCE | FIRE POWER / BASIC LOAD | SHOCK DELIVERY @ TARGET | TIME TO FIRE FIRST ROUND | GUN WEIGHT | AMMO WEIGHT | CONCEALABILITY | INHERENT SAFETY | MAINTENENCE FREEDOM | CARRYING EASE | AMMO PROCUREMENT / RELOADING EASE | EXPENSE OF PURCHASE / COST | EXPENSE OF OPERATION / ONGOING COST |
|---|---|---|---|---|---|---|---|---|---|---|---|---|---|---|---|---|---|
| **SHOTGUNS 131** | 7 | 10 | 9 | 6 | 6 | 9 | 8 | 8 | 7 | 3 | 6 | 7 | 9 | 8 | 9 | 10 | |
| Single/double | | 8 | | | | 6 | | | | | 6 | | 10 | | | 10 | |
| Pumps | | 9 | | | | 9 | | | | | 5 | | 9 | | | 9 | |
| Automatics | | 9 | | | | 9 | | | | | 5 | 6 | 7 | | 8 | 8 | |
| **RIFLES 123** | 10 | 8 | 8 | 7 | 5 | 7 | 8 | 7 | 7 | 5 | 5 | 9 | 8 | 7 | 7 | 8 | 7 |
| Manual actions | 10 | 8 | | | | 7 | | | | | | | 8 | | | 8 | 8 |
| Semi-auto | 9 | 7 | 8 | | | 7 | | | | | | | 6 | | | 7 | 5 |
| Full-auto | 9 | 6 | | | | 8 | | | | | | 6 | 4 | | | 4 | 4 |
| **PISTOLS 107** | 6 | 3 | 8 | 8 | 7 | 5 | 5 | 7 | 7 | 6 | 9 | 6 | 5 | 9 | 5 | 6 | 5 |
| Single actions | 7 | 4 | 7 | | | | 5 | | | | 7 | | 6 | 8 | | 7 | 6 |
| Double Actions | 6 | 3 | 8 | | | | 8 | | | | 9 | | 5 | 9 | | 5 | 5 |
| Autos (semi) | 6 | 2 | 8 | | | 7 | 4 | 7 | | | 10 | 5 | 4 | 10 | 3 | 5 | 4 |

## 1. AT WHAT RANGE WILL YOU BE SHOOTING?

Of course, you need to send a bullet to the target's location. Sometimes, that's a long shot; at other times, it's close. Range is the all- important factor. Any time you can fire on someone or something from a longer range than they can fire back or see you, you win.

In early military encounters, swords were better than knives, and spears were better than swords, and then bows and arrows were better than spears. Then, black powder made the tops of hills become choice military real estate because weapons of equal fire power gained a longer range advantage with height.  Today, ask the British.  The Argentine Air Force sank a ship with a French Exocet missile fired from forty miles out... England's electronic eyes couldn't see that far.

Since I have practiced long range shooting for a long time,  I like a "Bell telephone" gun--- one that lets all my targets know with feeling that "long distance is the next best thing to being there." Somehow, smacking a coyote 600 yards away just gives me that Dr Jekyl chuckle.

Of course, whatever you reach out and touch has to feel your influence.  Punching holes in paper with a .223 at five hundred yards is fine, but you don't get enough whump to demolish, especially with a 55 grain bullet.  To make a lasting  impression, you need at least a 65 grain bullet in 5.62, or the kind of cross-sectional density you find in a thirty caliber bullet.

As an added treat, I like a high ballistic coefficient, so my favorite long distance blaster is a boat tail, maybe with a banana peeling hollow point tip. That way, I not only smack my target, but the nose peels back and spins through the target like a buzz saw.

Naturally, smack goes both ways and converts on your shoulder to Ouch!  If you get so much ouch that your shooting efficiency drops, you will have to reduce the smack.  After recoil pads and a tighter sling haven't helped enough, you may have to go to a smaller caliber. Just make sure that whatever you settle on, you can shoot comfortably without being tempted to flinch.

Don't be afraid to go all the way down to a 22 rimfire.  Look at the good news:  You can carry five hundred rounds in your rucksack.  Lots of ammunition made for this weapon will get most jobs done.  Besides, starting out with this caliber has given lots of people the confidence to work up to heavier calibers.

From the chart, you can tell that rifles are great for range. As a next choice, pistols barely edge shotguns. Note the exception in the newer single shots, (Contenders), which reach out pretty well because they shoot rifle cartridges.

## 2. CAN YOU LOAD THE THING EASILY?

If you can't put gas in your car, it won't go. Guns are the same. If they take a ton of tedious procedure to load, you can't shoot them.

Of course, you carry a loaded weapon, but if you think you may need more than five shots, consider "down time," (time during which a weapon cannot be fired because it is being loaded). Shotguns are terrific because you merely stuff them with ammo, (on the run, if need be), and a cheap bandolier will practically drop fresh ammo in your hands. The new improvement with auto pistols is a flared magazine well---it guides the loaded clip into port.

Single action pistols can be kept full in a fire fight if you know the formula, "fire two, reload two". You come back with the hammer to half cock, and the old style (three screws) Ruger lines the cylinder port up with the ejection rod, so you go, "one out, one in." Incidentally, you should only need more than five shots if you're facing the Jesse James gang or you can't shoot. Practice.

## 3. CAN YOU SHOOT IT ACCURATELY?

Shooting mastery is extremely important. If you can't hit with it, don't buy it. I don't know why, but when the chips are down, as they are in Miami, everybody runs out to buy a magnum pistol. STUPID!

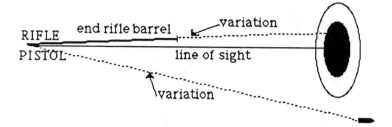

RIFLE — end rifle barrel — variation — line of sight

PISTOL — variation

Same variation, rifle above and pistol below. If you mis-align sights with your rifle, no big deal. But, mis-align with a pistol, and you miss the whole target.

Pistols are inherently poor (short sight base) at delivering precise bullet placement. Long hours of instruction and practice are required in order to hit any target with a hand held weapon (no shoulder support). Trigger pull straight to the rear is ultra-critical. Magnum power in a pistol compounds the problem, because the muzzle blast and kick can make a shooter shake, and thus create misses. Within range, a non-magnum caliber with the right bullet will perform just fine.

## TWO  PISTOL SIGHTS

Aligned

Disturbed; pulled to the right.

Slightly wrong here means way off target.

To understand another problem with pistols, you need to know the difference between:

**SIGHT ALIGNMENT**
**&**
**SIGHT PICTURE**

The former refers only to <u>precise</u> alignment of your sights. It's critical. The latter refers to where you put your <u>aligned</u> sights on the target. Any old place will do; a hit's a hit.

If your sights are aligned, you can wobble all over the target and score a hit whenever the hammer decides to fall. That's why you hear so much about "frame holds" in police work. The good guys are taught to align their sights and let one go anywhere through a door or window. On the other side of the coin, they never stand in a doorway--- they always burst into the room and get clear of that frame to keep from creating widows in their families.

pistol sight illustration--aligned, misaligned

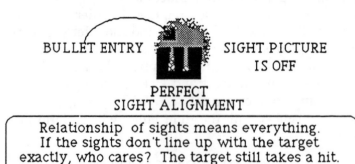

BULLET ENTRY          SIGHT PICTURE
                                    IS OFF

PERFECT
SIGHT ALIGNMENT

Relationship of sights means everything.
If the sights don't line up with the target
exactly, who cares? The target still takes a hit.

As I said, sight alignment is critical. If your sights are right, the weapon can wobble all over and you will still score a hit on your target. In othe rwords, you can let your arm move, but your wrist better stay locked and straight.

Focus on the front sight, and the rear
sight will look a little fuzzy, like this.

If you make a small alignment error rifles are forgiving; pistols ARE NOT. Minor errors in sight alignment are made negligible by a rifle's longer sight base. That's one reason why rifles are easier to master than pistols. Another reason is the steadying effect your shoulder support gives to the weapon.

So, if you ever decide to convert a shotgun to a shorter weapon so it can be used in tight places (indoors), make sure to add a folding stock when you replace the old stock with pistol grips. Thus, you can use the weapon as a pistol (wobbly) or a rifle (with shoulder support).

Winchoke Model 1200
Field Grade with Ventilated Rib

For shooting and loading mastery, shotguns are wonderful. Anytime you are blasting a bunch of lead balls into a three foot pattern, it's hard to miss any target, moving or still. The break-opens require down time for loading, but pumps and autos employ tubular magazines, (which you can extend on many models to hold 9 rounds.) If fire-fighting is the major purpose of your scattergun, buy a model that accepts shells while the bolt is closed so you can shove fresh fodder into the magazine while you are moving.

### 4. WILL IT COST A MINT?
How's your budget? Generally, shotguns are cheapest and pistols cost most. (See, SURVIVAL BUDGETING, BOOK I). Saturday Night Specials and some rimfire handguns are the cheap exception, but who, other than a pimp, wants to own one?

## 5. HOW ABOUT MAINTENANCE AND OPERATION COST?

After the purchase, shooting and maintenance cost money. Here again, shotguns are cheapest, unless you stick with rimfires. Rifle and pistol costs vary according to sub type. Since dirt in the action of some automatics is disastrous, you have to keep them sterile, and that takes a lot to time. On the other hand, dirt doesn't bother my single shot over/under too much. The last time I cleaned it, St Peter was a corporal.

## 6. CAN YOU HANDLE THE KICK?

If recoil is severe enough to make you flinch and thus disturb your aim, buy a smaller caliber. Where two people may be firing the same weapon, the smaller person decides this issue. Muzzle blast also makes a shooter flinch, so it's something to avoid.

## 7. DOES THE WEAPON HOLD
## ENOUGH BULLETS?

For the purposes of this chapter only, "basic load" is defined as how many rounds the weapon can shoot before reloading. It's the magazine or cylinder capacity. For a combatant, the higher the basic load, the better.

Firepower is our term for the number of rounds per minute. (RPM). A weapon with both excellent firepower and superior basic load allows you to smother a target with a quick cone of fire, thus insuring hit(s).

## 8. WILL THE TARGET FEEL YOUR INFLUENCE?

The farther away from the muzzle, the less smack you deliver because air resistance slows bullets down. Shock delivery refers to how severely the struck target is affected by bullet impact. At close range, shotguns win in this catagory because of the tremendous blow-out delivered by the heavy load of lead, most of which stops in the target. But, at long distance, (more than a hundred yards away), a shotgun loses its clout. Rifles do better than pistols because of heavier bullet weight and higher speed.

Speaking about shock, I used to know a salesman who swore by the power of the .45 Colt automatic. "Shocking power. That's the whole deal," he said. "The big 220 grain bullets stop in the target's body, and transfer all the bullet's shock power." I believed...

## WHAT'S NEW IN PISTOL CALIBERS?

Since we published this book, new pistol calibers hit the market and created a lot of stir--- notably, the 10 mm. I talked to a Remington representative at the SHOT (Shooting, Hunting, Outdoor Trade; not open to public) show in New Orleans.

Basically, he told me this. The cartridge was originally developed through the FBI after they conducted an infamous shootout with some bad guys down in Florida. The cartridge was the bureau's answer to agents who couldn't shoot. (Sort of like replacing the typewriter for authors who can't spell.)

As we all know, lots manufacturers made new guns. *Miami Vice* cops showed off the hardware. Ammunition stayed priced at the Rolls Royce level. What's the bottom line? Forget it.

Listen to the words of Craig Huber, who will soon publish a self defense manual for this publisher. "Stick with your .45; just add a few bells and whistles." For human targets, that's a good way to go.

Then, a few years back, we tree'd a two year old black bear about 70 yards away from the muzzle of my Colt Commander. I blasted, but the only shock around was the shock I was in as it snarled out of that tree! She charged hard and tore up the dogs before Jim Minter killed her. Nobody noticed I got scared except the guy who did my laundry. After a little autopsy, I discovered my slug buried in a thick layer of the bear's underskin fat. I traded the gun off.

11

## 10. DO YOU HAVE TO GO THROUGH A LOT OF TROUBLE TO FIRE IT?

A quick first round is important; a lot of contests are won by causing another bullet to finish second in a field of two. If you ever surprise a snake or a bear with cubs in the woods just once, you will thank God for your fast draw pistol. Shotgunners can shoot faster than rifle shooters because they can bring their weapons on target without having to look through sights. So, if you want to be super-quick---scatter some shot. If you cut the barrel on your shotgun, it becomes even quicker, but the range shortens, and the weapon will no longer produce good patterns. Also, you can replace the stock with a pistol grip and gain speed, but you lose shoulder-bridge stability, so accuracy will suffer.

## 11&12. DO YOU NEED TO BE A PACK MULE TO CARRY IT?

Gun weight and ammo weight are both unimportant if you travel by horse, boat or vehicle. If you walk a lot, however, lighter is better because tired survivors make mistakes. Since the .223 cartridge weighs less than the .30 caliber, you can carry more rounds and thus increase firepower (quantity) with the lighter weight.

## 13. WHEN YOU CARRY IT, DOES THE WHOLE WORLD NOTICE?

concealability from holsters

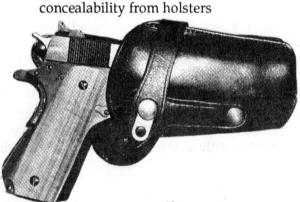

Shotguns can also be modified for concealability. Some beaurocrat decided to make the world a safer place---so shotgun barrels shorter than 18 inches are a no-no. Now only criminals who are out on parole cut them any shorter.

Bull-pups are great rifles if you have to conceal one. The action is contained in the stock, so that you get a much shorter weapon with the same length barrel.

## 14. WILL BUYING AMMUNITION PUSH YOU INTO BANKRUPTCY?

I owned a Savage in a weird big-bore caliber once. The factory ammo cost a dollar a round. Needless to say, I bought reloading dies immediately. For survival rifles, stick with military calibers. The government creates tons of ammo, which tips the economic scales of supply and demand in your favor.

To become an expert with any weapon, you need to practice, and burning gunpowder costs money. With centerfire cartridges, you get around the expense by reloading, which can be an enjoyable past time. It costs money to buy and store all the equipment, so lots of shooters burn cheaper rimfire powder to learn sighting, breathing, and trigger control. However, learning about big bore noise and recoil still requires blasting away with the real McCoy, so plan on spending some spare time reloading.

Pistol rounds are expensive and harder to reload than rifle cartridges. Crimping a pistol case is tedious, and you use three dies (rather than two for rifle) to complete the round. Unlike most rifle cartridges, a pistol case will accept a double powder charge, and the resulting explosion will ruin your whole day. On the other hand, shotgun rounds are cheap and any sloppy reloader can do an adequate job.

The no-deposit, no-return variety of ammunition is looking better than ever these days. Both weapons and ammunition are cheap, and the low recoil, minor noise, and logistics are also attractive. The cartridges are available everywhere, cost less than big bore brass, and you can carry a thousand rounds with little trouble. Since a rimfire hardly recoils, the weapons can be lighter. I have one that floats, takes down to fit in my backpack, shoots accurately, and puts out lead in a semi-automatic hurry. Shock power is improved with the new high velocity ammo.

### 15. MIGHT THIS WEAPON KILL YOU?

Think of safety. How easy is it to shoot---yourself or a bystander? Nobody ever thinks he/she is an un-safe gunner. Still, hundreds of deaths and injuries are caused by careless weapon handling. Because I was once a hunter safety instructor in California, I read the accidents reports regularly. One hunter was killed by his dog, who, quite naturally, was licking the salt off the trigger on a loaded shotgun which was standing in the back seat of the hunter's car.

Automatic pistols are safety's worst, primarily because of the clip removal, round-still- in-the-chamber problem. The 45 autos are famous for killing friends and relatives. In Germany, a lieutenant on overnight CQ duty took his magazine out and blew a hole in a wall with the round he forgot in the chamber. I know this because he got me out of bed at 0400 to help patch the wall. Another time, a kid I had housed in my basement did the same and blew a hole in my banjo. That was OK, though, I still had him to pick on.

Have adjustable sights put on here.

**Sterling 45 Auto**
**Model 450**
**Double Action**

If you must go pistol and you like Automatic, get a double action. You will pay through the nose, but you can get the first round off much quicker.    14

Shotguns are rated slightly more dangerous than rifles, because once accidentally discharged, spread shot will destroy a lot more than a single bullet might. Had the lieutenant been playing with his shotgun, I wouldn't have patched a hole; I would have hung a window in it.

## 16. WILL IT STILL FUNCTION IF I NEGLECT IT...?

Or is it like a wife? If you are busy all the time, maintenance will be a bother. You need it to work for you, faithfully, on a minute's notice. But you may be busy, and if your weapon won't shoot unless it's freshly groomed, (tight tolerance auto pistols and some gas-operated shotguns) don't marry it.

## 17. HOW EASY IS THIS THING TO CARRY?

Finally, think about carrying. Pistols are easiest; you can do all kinds of activity and always have one handy. Shotguns and rifles are more troublesome. Rifles require careful handling; knocking them around carelessly can destroy the weapon's zero.

*****

When you use the chart, apply only the attributes you want. For example, if you weigh 250 pounds and are deaf, you won't worry about recoil and noise; disregard these qualities when you add up the numbers.

I applied all of the attributes, so my three basic weapon totals are: shotguns prove to be best with 131 points; rifles follow with 123; and pistols trail way behind.

If you have unlimited funds, you may be thinking about a full automatic weapon. After all, we see UZI's and AR 16's tear up the bad guys every day on TV.

DON'T GO FOR IT.

Automatics shoot a lot of misses. Because of recoil, they climb, and shoot over everything. They consume hundreds of pounds of ammo, which you have to carry, so you're weighted down and you can't maneuver. I shot a Browning Automatic Rifle many years ago, and it was so much better on semi- auto that I seldom switched. Stick with a weapon that requires aim for every shot. Just squeeze the trigger faster; you'll be potent.

# Shot Sizes

As numbers increase, shot size gets smaller.

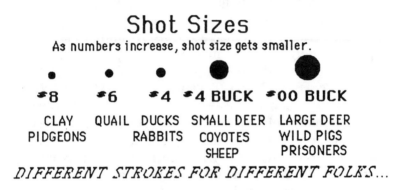

| #8 | #6 | #4 | #4 BUCK | #00 BUCK |
|----|----|----|---------|----------|
| CLAY PIDGEONS | QUAIL | DUCKS RABBITS | SMALL DEER COYOTES SHEEP | LARGE DEER WILD PIGS PRISONERS |

*DIFFERENT STROKES FOR DIFFERENT FOLKS...*

In shotgun selection, the first factor is recoil. If you can't take the kick, go with a lesser guage or a lighter powder load (if reloading). You're pretty much limited to either a 12 or 20 guage, and the smaller twenty will furnish you with plenty of power if you use three inch magnums. Likewise, you can lighten your custom loads for the twelve and save some shoulder bruises.

Pumps or autos? Pump action shotguns are cheaper and more reliable, but some police departments have dumped them because shucking them exposes the shooter to incoming fire. Better yet, automatics load themselves, and do it reliably <u>if you keep them reasonably clean.</u>

Both pumps and auto's can be adapted to shorter stocks, pistol grips, and 25-shot cylinder magazines. In addition to gauge and type, you should consider ammunition. From tiny BB's to larger buckshot, you get a special effect for any occasion. As the shot size increases, so does all- important range.

For $500-$800, a survival rifle in either of two calibers, .223 or .308 is probably best because those calibers are used by the military, so ammo is cheap and easy to find. Another good military rifle is the M-1 Garand (in 30-06). I shot a Garand for years; it was great. Some people complain about the eight shot clip, but I liked that too. When the last round is fired, the spring clip twangs away and the bolt stays to the rear, so you're ready for quick reload. (Incidentally, the world's best gun deal is occasionally available from DCM, Director of Civilian Marksmanship, Wash. D.C. They sell an M-1 Garand for only $165.

On the other hand, box magazine rifles haven't been that kind to me. Many of them finish firing in the Gomer-Pyle-empty mode, (surprise, surprise, surprise), with bolt forward. Bad news. You have to remove one box, insert another, and crank on the bolt handle to get a new round into the chamber before you start serving customers again. During all of that down time you're sure to draw incoming fire. The remedy: Start your loading with about four tracers, (first loaded/last fired) so you get advance notice before firing dry.

Even with its drawbacks, the H&K 91 is very popular. One of the gunners on my team swore by it. For me though, it's uncomfortable to shoot because of the pistol grip, which precludes a thumb-wrap spotweld. Just for the way I shoot and the positions I shoot from, my M1-A shoots tighter groups. Still, the H&K has some great features: The zero adjustment on the peep sight beats memory by a bunch. Also, it functions fine when dirty, because of the fluted chambers. I hear complaints about the flutes tearing up the brass, but we get up to seven reloads out of the shell cases anyway.

Thirty caliber is fine for just about everything. You can use 110 gr. bullets that will flat out scream for short distances (300 yds), or you can load a 200 grain choo-choo that will keep on chugging through bushes, leaves and light obstacles. The in-between choices are vast, offering weights and velocities for every need.

My favorite .30 caliber bullet is a banana peeler in 165 grain boat tail. Boat tails have rear ends like a submarine, so they maintain good velocity (ballistic coeficient is .477) all the way to the target. Thus, they shoot flat, reaching out to 500 yards in .67 of a second. At that distance the bullet smacks with a velocity of 1800 feet per second, (like a close-in 30/30 shot). What's more, the jacket of the bullet is machined so that it peels back on all sides like a banana, leaving spinning, ragged edges to buzz saw through target meat. Lots of other .30

caliber bullets do great things  also, so this is a good survival choice.

Currently, I am into the lightweight, lots'o ammo thing, so I use a .223 caliber.  Mine is a Ruger (love his guns!) Mini-14 in stainless.  No, I haven't bought the automatic kit!  As you probably have heard, you can buy the parts to convert this to a full automatic. Automatics are illegal, but the parts to make them that way can be sold through magazines with ease. Beaurocrats!

Recoil on a .223 is negligible.  Trajectory is flat. It's accurate.  It just isn't a long distance smacker, although it will hit at 500 yds and wound.

Incidentally, most survivalists talk about one weapon for hunting big game, another for small game, a carry-around gun, and a GTW, (go-to-war).  I don't buy it.  I like one rifle, maybe two.  I used to go to gun shows three or four times a year and trade around a lot, so I've owned one of everything.  I spent a lot of time working with them, but I couldn't keep up.

The trajectory nomographs were different, and I frequently became confused about elevation until I scoped (20 power) out a few rounds.  Book I of this series teaches how to graph bullet flight; it's a critical skill.

A weapon should be like a wife; once you choose, that's what you marry and go to bed with. Don't mess around; it only screws your mind up.  Also, you need to know a lot of things about your weapon that only experience and constant close familiarity will teach you, so banging something else only serves to steal your mind away from business.  Just as in life, you'll never be a straight shooter if you change around all the time.

So, I am in favor of using one weapon for hunting, plinking, target, and companion. Choose it and use it---you'll become the same kind of pro that Eskimos are. They kill just about everything with .22 long rifle shells.

Just as in shotgun selection, you're looking for a bullet you can shoot without getting so nervous (from either muzzle blast or recoil), that you disturb sight alignment as the firing pin strikes. Then tune up with hand loaded ammo, carefully put together, and record your reloads AND their performance until you get it to shoot with fine, confidence-building precision.

### SIGHTING SYSTEMS

On whatever weapon you choose, make sure the sights will work for you. On a winter overcast day, it's just too dark to use some of my open sights. You absolutely need a set of sights that work for you in all kinds of weather.

That means: A) enough side relief (space on either side of the blade) to enable you to align your sights in poor light, and B), a front blade that is flat on top so you can align it straight across the top of your leaf. Manufacturers should learn that.

My big bore .358 has a little tiny round bead on the blade and a half moon leaf that I never could get right. I finally flattened the top of that blade so it aligns for elevation. Windage (side-to-side sight alignment) is still hard to achieve on that rifle. Even in sunlight, I am forced to waste a lot of time and concentration sighting on a target. On moving targets, I've lost shots...

Error city

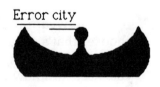

File the blade and rear sights flat for easy line-up

The gunmakers also need to to learn another critical lesson. Just like animal predators, human predators will hunt for plunder at night, also.

Therefore, a survivalist has much better than 50/50 chance of using his weapon in the dark. In Book I, we taught the "Platform Accuracy, Unitized Level" system for night shooting. This method enables you to "feel it" when your weapon is level, and line up a fluorescent line on the top of your barrel with the shadow of the target. Thus, you can hit accurately without needing sights.

Modify your open sights with two colors of fluorescent paint brushed on the back side of the blade and leaf, respectively. Then, you hold your weapon under a poncho and charge your sights with a penlight. In this way, you save your night vision, but your sights are visible to you. You'll be able to line your weapon up on the faintest shadow.

Scopes are fine in daylight, of course, unless it rains all day and the scope fogs. That's the reason you should mount a scope in such a way that you can use your metal sights when weather turns against you. One company now makes a scope with metallic sights attached to the top of it. Good deal.

## BORROWING FROM ONE WEAPON
## FOR ANOTHER

Many rifles lend themselves to weapon attributes combinations. Ruger's Mini-14 can be pistol stocked and performs nicely that way if you spray 'n pray. Its peep sights are difficult to use if the weapon isn't shouldered.

Another combo is the .30 caliber carbine with paratrooper stock; in tight quarters it's a pistol; extend the stock and it's a rifle. I just never liked that .30 carbine bullet, though. A Korean war veteran told me he shot an enemy soldier 11 times, and the guy kept coming! That suggests a little to be desired in the knock-down department.

One of my favorites for hunting is a combination rifle/shotgun, with a 30/30 rifle over 20 gauge. The 30/30 reaches out accurately and the shotgun blasts birds and close-in targets. Recently, I saw my shotgun load of #4's spread out and catch a coyote as he screamed through the woods. After that, I switched to the top barrel and made a careful, killing shot with the 30/30.

Now they sell Accelerators (available in stores) which are 55 grain bullets wrapped in thirty caliber plastic. The plastic flies off just outside the muzzle, and you send a .223 round down range at roughly 3,000 fps. Result: By changing shells you can reach out with a flat trajectory or use a heavy, knock-down smacker for bigger game.

Carry two guns (rifle/pistol) if you like, but combine them so one shoots heavy ammo and the other light. If your shoulder gun is big bore, your sidearm should be rimfire. This way, you have utility.

Yes, pistols do have their place. The brush in my country is too thick for carrying a rifle, so I holster a .357 mag, which I recently used with some success on a bear's face.

Every so often you need to use both hands, as when you dig a ditch, hammer a nail, or fish. At a time like that, a pistol can be a blessing.

Three basic kinds of pistols are available (excluding Contenders). They are automatics, and single or double action revolvers. We call a pistol automatic, even though we have to pull the trigger for each shot. With a quick trigger finger, simply draw, and spray lead all over your target. Some pistols box-style magazines hold over a dozen rounds. That's the good news. The bad news is about cleanliness and malfunction. If you don't keep some autos clean, they won't feed. Then they're useless.

Revolvers are more reliable. The cyclinder turns mechanically so the new round lines up with the hammer. Autos pull all kinds of dirty tricks; they fail to feed, or stove-pipe and jam. They also shoot mightier bullets, such as the magnums, .41, and .44, although new automatics will pump these monsters. They just kick like a mule.

Solve the safety problem in your six- shooter by loading only five rounds. You can't shoot a double action revolver while the cyclinder is swing out, and the down time could be dangerous. Singles, on the other hand, can be constantly loaded as you fire. I sold an article in the 1981 <u>AMERICAN HANDGUNNER ANNUAL</u> that teaches you how to reload a single as you fire, thus avoiding down time. In a fire fight, if you even suspect that you're up against a shot-counter, shoot six as you reload, then take careful aim with number seven while your adversary changes position.

With the chart, you'll be able to choose a survival weapon custom tailored to your needs. Once you have done that, apply the other principles and you will have the ideal caliber or gauge. Then, you're ready to practice with your chosen weapon until you can make it speak the universal survival language--in a most persuasive manner.

# Chapter 2

Staying alive through the fine art of...

## COMBAT GUNNERY

Anyone who has been here on earth for more than a few decades can tell you: "We are going downhill."

From the time we put together the first edition of this book until now, things have gotten worse. So, sooner or later, you'll probably have to defend yourself against an armed attacker(s). Therefore, you should learn how to shoot a weapon in the combat mode.

Current instruction on survival combat gunnery is sparse. Most shooting instructors teach you:

A. How to shoot a weapon, by yourself, in daylight. That's OK, but it doesn't begin to approach the kinds of problems you will probably encounter.

B. To shoot against an adversary who is armed with a weapon similar to yours. That's not OK. DON'T YOU EVER...! engage in a fight where the odds are 50/50. Also, it's a safe bet the other side will probably understand the stupidity of a 50/50 fight, so, most likely, you'll be out-gunned.

STAY ALIVE. If you stay alive and uninjured, you win the battle. In Book I of this series, Rick Woodcroft teaches you the principles in "Hand-to- hand combat." He teaches you not to try too hard by over-extending because you risk taking some damaging counter-punches while you're off balance and out of position. Weapons conflicts are the same, but a counter-punch shooter will do a lot more than damage.

If it even looks like you may get shot at, wear Kevlar, especially around your head and torso. They also make Kevlar underwear, but if I took a direct hit in the groin with a high velocity round, I think I would rather die. (just kidding).

MANEUVER AND SHOOT ACCORDING TO THE PROBABLE DURATION OF THE FIGHT. What's the status of law enforcement in your area? Without police protection (and there may not be much) you'll have to duke it out and win---or die. As it is today, however, you will most likely get some help from a superior armed force (like police). In that event, you only have to fight a holding action, and you want to stay alive and stay out of jail.

So, don't shoot anybody, if you can help it. I am amazed at how the law changes from state to state. In many states, you can only shoot if there is a "clear and present danger." In others, anybody in your house is fair game, and some police officers have advocated shooting somebody, then dragging their dead carcass inside.

That's stupid. Any warm animal with a hole in it will always bleed, and even a mediocre investigator will find the blood track. On the other hand, even if you drop a burglar in the house, and he has one of your butcher knives in his hand, your legal position will improve a lot.

No matter what you do, DON'T MAKE ANY STATEMENT after the shoot. Call an attorney immediately, or have a friend stay with you, and SAY NOTHING. I have interviewed numerous policemen, some high ranking, and most with over 10 years on the force, and they all agree, "Lawyers lie." Criminal law encounters are contests between a defense attorney, who is motivated by money, and a prosecutor, who is motivated by conviction statistics. Don't confuse them with facts. I know personally of one case in which a shooter was tape recorded and said, "It was an accident." The written report read, "I shot him on purpose after he put his hands up." Then the tape was "accidentally" erased when a defense attorney asked for it. DON'T SAY ONE WORD---TO ANYBODY.

KNOW YOUR WEAPON. Is the weapon zeroed? How far out can you shoot effectively? What kinds of barricades will your bullets pierce? How many rounds will your weapon hold?

KNOW WHAT YOU'RE UP AGAINST. Special Forces 1st Lieutenant Nick Rowe got into a fight with some Vietnamese. He should have known he was up against a superior force because he captured an NVA weapon. Nevertheless, he pursued, was ambushed, caught, and captured. Read his, Five Years to Freedom. He made a critical error in failing to assess his enemy. Go thou, and do un-likewise.

Learn to listen carefully to the sounds of incoming gun fire. Rifles bang, big bores boom, and pistols crack. From the sound, you can tell what kind of lead is chasing you, and develop a plan accordingly.

SET UP AND CONTROL THE TACTICAL SITUATION IN YOUR FAVOR. Make him move through lighted areas; you stay in the dark. In hostile turf, never stare into a light source (fire, headlights), with both eyes open. Close one eye or wear an eye patch (removeable) so that you don't get into a fire- fight with night blindness. It takes about a half hour for your eyes to adjust. Try it. In the dark, close and cover one eye, then stare with the other into the light. Then look into the dark, and switch-wink your eyes. (Open left, close right; then, opposite). The covered eye will see, the other is night-blind.

In daylight, put the sun at your back to blind him, or at night, the moon behind him to make his silhouette an easy target. Wait for them to expose themselves before firing. Get above them if appropriate. If you are being shot at, think about torching a fire to their area (downwind). Don't get trapped. NEVER move into a dead-end area.

DIVERSIFY. Carry a variety of ammunition. For a revolver, you might start with a couple of shot loads, then a pair of hollow points, and finally, two swaged semi-wadcutters for penetration.

The variety of ammo available for shotguns is practically endless. Of course, carry slugs. Double aught buck is great for spreading your influence over a wider area, and you can custom load with a dime and shot combo. (The shot smacks and the dime cuts right on through.) In Phoenix, Ariz., Accuracy Systems makes stinger shot (rubber pellets) and Thunderflash, which travels about a hundred yards and explodes with a stunning boom.

A broad range of problems can be handled with different rifle rounds. Accelerators double the speed and shoot flat (leaving no marks on the bullet). FMJ rounds are penetrators, and BTHPBP's make your day by travelling great distances (boat tails) to tear up (hollow point banana peelers) whatever they smack.

In what sequence should you load these different rounds? The key word to remember is LIFO, which stands for Last-In-First-Out. Most rifles, shotguns and pistols employ a tubular or box magazine.

The last round loaded will be the first shot. Take note of the terrain in which you operate and figure out at what distance the most likely first contact range will be; then load accordingly.

If you reload shotshells, you can use flechettes (cut pieces of #12 guage copper wire) to make a round that will not penetrate a household wall or load double-aught buck that will go right on through. They also make shot shell loads for pistols. Load these last so they shoot out first if you are worried about running into snakes. Lightweight hollow points produce better muzzle velocities, and they break up in a target so that ALL of the bullet's shocking power is transferred.

## GENERAL WEAPONS MATCH-UPS

Let's examine each type of weapon from a tactical standpoint. Firearms are like chess pieces. Each has strengths; each has weaknesses. To win, you match your weapon's strengths against opponent's weaknesses. A .357 mag may beat four aces, but against a shotgun forget the game and leave. Against a rifle, leave quicker, and pray as you go.

If you exclude automatics, weapons encounters occur in one of three flavors according to this diagram:

| YOUR WEAPON | THEIRS |
|---|---|
| Pistol | Pistol |
| Rifle | Rifle |
| Shotgun | Shotgun |

## YOUR PISTOL

You learned earlier that pistols are the worst survival weapon. Yet most of the combat books published deal with <u>hand</u> gunnery, because law enforcement officers are the primary market. Living outdoors in a survival situation is different, and long guns can really enhance your LIVING, LIFE style. But--- since most people own a handgun first, and since they are convenient to carry, you may get caught in a fire fight with only your pistol. Should that happen, pray first. Then understand that what you've seen on TV is Hollywood showbiz, and it just won't work in real life.

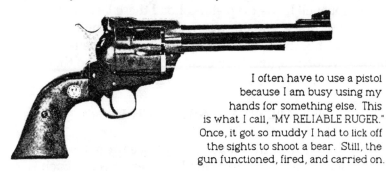

I often have to use a pistol because I am busy using my hands for something else. This is what I call, "MY RELIABLE RUGER." Once, it got so muddy I had to lick off the sights to shoot a bear. Still, the gun functioned, fired, and carried on.

Pistols are concealable, easy to draw and fire first (quick-shoot situations), effective for SHORT ranges, and more adaptable to indoor combat. However, they are vulnerable to any superior range weapon. Therefore, getting into a bullet exchange against any other weapon could ruin your whole day unless the range happens to be short, and you get the first fast round off.

PISTOL vs PISTOL. Why should you EVER get into any combat where the chances of you winning or losing are 50/50? I won't even fist fight that way, and gunfights are rather terminal events for the loser. Above all, you had better know what your range limits are. Measure your shot groups at various distances. In combat, figure that you will shoot another 30% wider. If your adversary shoots better, either because of personal ability or a longer barrel (sight base), you have a serious problem on your hands.

Get some help, if you can. Don't be a (dead) hero. If you can't get help, back out of the conflict carefully, until the range is longer than either pistol can shoot effectively. In most police/criminal shoots, the cop is outgunned. See, the ACLU has fixed things by lawsuit so the best any cop can use is a +P load out of a 38 Special.

The slime of our society doesn't have to follow public policy, so you may find yourself up against a 41 mag auto. You need to confine this customer, but at what risk? Don't expose yourself, and remember: "Your new car warranty does not cover magnum bullet holes." Don't hide behind the door.

Learn to avoid down time. Speed loaders for double action revolvers, or a spare hand with ready clips for an automatic are mandatory. Don't buy an auto that empties with the slide forward. That means you have to change clips and noisely jack a new round into the chamber.

YOUR PISTOL vs HIS RIFLE. This is a Biblical match up. You're David and the rifleman is Goliath. Unless you happen to be closer than 25 yds, you had better be barricaded better than a tank crew. Rifle rounds go through cars, doors, walls, and a .30 FMJ (Full Metal Jacket) round will go through a tree a foot thick. Many .30 caliber riflemen carry armor-piercing bullets (black tips).

---

### POLICE URBAN FIREFIGHT GUIDE

Once barricaded, don't move unless he moves and gets a better position on you. Don't fire first; draw fire as long as you're secure. Why? The first guy to shoot in a firefight discloses his position and tells the other (if he knows his business) what kind of firepower is chasing him. Once somebody knows what they're up against, they can move to adjust range and then fire for effect.

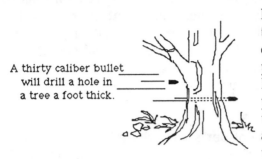

A thirty caliber bullet will drill a hole in a tree a foot thick.

If it ever happens that the situation is do or die, and you face a rifle, I hate to tell you, but you will have to advance within your weapon's shooting range. That range will also be well within his. Assuming you are in top physical shape, and you have lots of good cover to hide behind as you move in, you might make it...

YOUR PISTOL vs HIS SHOTGUN. I would rather play against the Dallas Cowboys without padding. A modified shotgun (short barrelled, pistol-gripped) is just about as quick as any pistol, and it will blow you away. Doc Holiday understood this at the OK corral. Going up against a shotgun with a pistol in the open is brave stupidity. Up against a rifle, you might make it when you close range (so that your pistol will be effective). But a shotgunner spreads out a pattern with much better chances of nailing you.

In outdoor terrain, you can fight a decent holding action if you get to higher ground and you're barricaded. HOLD tightly (against a support), expose almost nothing, and SHOOT CAREFULLY.

YOUR SHOTGUN
Would you like to expand your unpopularity? Buy a shotgun.

Every time you pull the trigger, you create a wide cone of fire, and any target in the cone will feel your influence. If you wish to reach farther out but not as wide, change the choke on the end of the barrel.

**Shotguns pattern:**
Wide with an improved cyclinder choke,
Medium spread with a modfied choke, and,
Narrow with a full choke.
As the pattern narrows, range extends.

## SHOTGUN CHOKE EFFECTS
### Range shortens as the pattern spreads

full choke

**55 yds**

modified choke

**40 yds**

improved cylinder

**30 yds**

A rifled slug will produce good accurate range out of a shotgun, but you don't get that happy spread out pattern---just one slug.   (Curved air vanes on the slug's side make it revolve for accuracy.)

### YOUR SHOTGUN vs HIS PISTOL
As they say in tennis, "You're advantage."   But that doesn't mean you are going to win the match.

You need to keep a hundred yards away because very few people can put a pistol round on target at that distance.   On the other hand, you are guaranteed some kind of hit.  Use double 00 buck.  Wound anything you can, horse, car, boat; then punch through to destroy the invader with a rifled slug.

Shotguns are great for responding to close ambush. The shot spread compensates for a lack of pinpoint accuracy by saturating any target area with fast-flying lead. That's super at night because it's hard to aim any weapon in the dark. As we taught you in Book I, use a PAUL stance to keep the weapon level and fluorescent colored tape or paint on top of the barrel (rib) to enable you to line the weapon up from side to side. Then, blast.

However, against a pistol, close in, standing up and firing like that wouldn't be my preference, because you expose too much of a target (your body). Several pistols shoot about a time and a half as fast as shotguns. In addition, the bulkier shot doesn't penetrate anything as well as one, smooth, pointed projectile. Thus, if you are standing behind an interior wall, (one and a half inches of gypsum drywall), a lucky pistolier could smoke you. Hint: stay low, and don't make noise.

Shotguns are also vulnerable to long range attack in an open area. Because they shoot round shot, wind resistance causes them not to maintain velocity like an aero-dynamically shaped bullet. No velocity = no smack; shotguns don't deliver power at a distance. The shotgun's advantage consist of nine rounds with every trigger pull, and the rifleman or pistolero shoots only one. Of course, it only takes one to finish you, so a great idea is to turn yourself into the smallest target possible. Do this by shooting from the prone position, and rolling to keep on the move.

YOUR SHOTGUN vs HIS RIFLE  You will have to make some quick adjustments in order to bring the tactical situation into your advantage.

Switch to slugs or close the range. If you can't do either of those, get well barricaded. Move only when 100% sure of safety. Should you pick up incoming while in open country, get into cover immediately. If you run into boulders and rocks, you may have a lot of ricochets looking for you. Should that happen, incidentally, cover yourself with some of the smaller rocks you run into, or even use the shotgun stock to cover your chest area. You'll be uncomfortable, guaranteed, but cool it; night time will come soon, and then it's your turn to move in close and even the score.

SHOTGUN vs SHOTGUN. Why get into a 50/50 shoot out when you could lose your life? Let a few loads fly, and then get out of the encounter as soon as it's safe. Outcome here depends on superior loads, luck or exposure. It could go either way.

### YOUR RIFLE

Finally, we discuss a combat weapon that makes sense. I love a rifle. Hopefully, you and your pet firearm have been shooting tight groups, which means you can nestle into position and blast anything from +500 yards.

RIFLES are long range shooters, but they require CAREFUL sighting. Given the right ammo, rifles will punch through lots of barricades. Rifles are vulnerable, however, to close-quarter ambush, and they are unwieldy indoors. If a rifle is your only home defense and someone invades, slip outdoors and guard the entrance or wait for a light to go on.

Defending with a rifle is like patrolling in the Navy. Just as an aircraft carrier always travels with company, rifles should always be accompanied by shotgun destroyers.  If you patrol a lot, use the buddy system; each of you carries a different weapon.  That way, the shotgunner handles short range targets.

Shooting long distance with a rifle really improves with a separate shooting scope for reading the wind and seeing precise detail.  In Book I, we detailed ways to read the wind with a separate spotting scope, so you can slide a bullet through a tough crosswind and smack a target 1,000 yards away.

I've shot .22 rifles 300 yards away and scored on cottontails ONLY BECAUSE I was able to scope out my first bullet landing, hold carefully, and then correct the next round.

Any second person on your shooting team can do the same for you.  They see the bullet strike and give you an immediate correction, such as: "Down two feet, left three feet," so the next round splatters your target.

RIFLE vs RIFLE.  It would seem at first to be an even fight.  Not always.  With rifles, caliber, shooter ability, sighting systems and bullet type make a lot of difference.

Listen carefully to the guns that are firing from the other side.  If you're hearing the crack of a small bore centerfire, and you own a big bore bullet pusher, the relative energies give you an edge at long distance. So, open the range, and then open fire.

Most probably you'll be facing more than one pistol shooter.  If they're gunfight-smart, they will move towards you.  Keep them out of pistol range and move back as you pick your shots.  Going to high ground is a good idea, but only if you already have more than 150 yards distance on them.  One will fire as the other moves.  That's because your movement up the side of a mountain exposes you.  Expect to hear some extra noise; once they see you, everybody will get excited and shoot all at the same time.  Once out of range, however, the game is yours.  You shoot a bullet two and a half times as fast as theirs, and your accuracy is much better.  Granted, both sides can move without detection at a distance.  However, if your rifle is scoped, you can pick up on shadows as well as outlines in the brush, and remember, you have great (FMJ) penetrating, as well as ricochet power.

YOUR RIFLE vs HIS SHOTGUN.  Likewise, against a shotgun, move away.  If he has slugs, move 300 yards away in order to enjoy life.  Be a lot less bold in movement.  In old war movies you see marines running zig-zag patterns with rifle fire landing all around them.  Maybe.  If you find yourself outside of Hollywood but inside somebody's shotgun range and you run through any open ground, they will have you for dinner.  If you are being chased, open the range by moving DOWNHILL.  Low ground for a rifleman is perfect when you have a shotgunner at the top of the hill standing up to look for you.  Remember the bullet drop rule, (Book I) and just aim a little high...

Carry what you know works.  Just as you put on a raincoat before you go into the weather, get ready for danger with the appropriate weapon and a wide variety of ammunition.

In combat gunnery it will seldom be a one on one proposition.  Humans are a gregarious lot, and they form all kinds of groups and clubs for noble purposes.  If the purpose is immoral and violent, we call their group a gang.  That's probably what you'll be facing.  What will they will be like?

Most of these people will be under-educated, slow-to-think types who are alive because they compensated for stupidity by becoming street-wise and ruthless.  As always, a gang has more power than the individuals who make it up.  Under- estimating them would be a mistake.

They won't give up. They can't. They are ruled by pride, and they would rather die brave than live as cowards. They have lived in fear of dying all their lives and have adjusted; you cannot intimidate them. Once committed to taking your property or your family, they won't back off.

Here's proof: In Los Angeles last year, there were more than 700 homicides (two per day). Over half occurred on gang turf. Other major cities are pretty much the same. On L.A. freeways, 18 people came up casualties as a result of gunshot wounds. How many people do you guess now carry guns in their cars? I guess thousands.

The question isn't how able they are to shoot, it's how avail-able. So---if you get into combat gunnery, you will need a team (unless you are Rambo and own an M-60 machine gun.) In Book I, we taught you how to form a survival team. If you did that, then it will be your team against their gang, and you will powder them.

Just train to shoot as a co-ordinated team. You no longer shoot or think as individuals. Work it out so that you don't have everyone empty their weapons all at once. Fire in sequence. This way, you always have a weapon loaded, and you can respond to opportunity.

Standardize your calibers so that everyone shoots the same caliber. You need shotguns, small bore and big bore rifles. Pistols are a secondary consideration, but if you must, stick to 9mm and shoot 110 gr hollow points.

First and foremost, TAKE GOOD COVER. We want zero exposure. If nobody gets hurt on either side, but they shoot the daylights out of your house, you win, because they go away telling themselves they won, which means they probably won't need to prove anything with a re-match.

In all your encounters, place big and small bore shooters side by side. You need to achieve the ability to cover long range with accuracy and short range with devastating firepower. That means: big .30 calibers paired with shotguns. Shotgunners scope, help, and pass ammunition but don't shoot until the range closes.

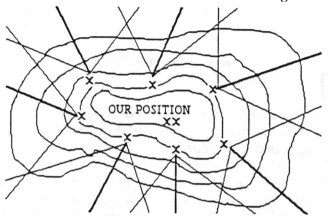

Reaching out to 1,000 yards from "x" marked positions with overlapping fields of fire.

Out in the woods, you may need to maneuver. If cover permits. Several shoot while one guy moves. A fire team leader assigns fields of fire so you have a slight overlap. You cover your area much the same as a basketball team playing a zone defense. Talk to each other. Everybody stays informed, and the morale stays up when you chatter back and forth.

### CAR TO CAR COMBAT

The bumper sticker in L.A. reads, "Keep honking; I'm reloading." So it's a good idea to know something about car-to-car combat. As you've probably noticed, the front and rear windows of almost all vehicles don't open, so you can't shoot out of them unless you first shoot them out. That means most shooting, both outbound and incoming, will be done out of side windows.

The first step, therefore, is to smoke your windows. You need to use the darkest you can find, so nobody can see who you are or where you are. This is especially important  if your wife or sister will be driving; they are more likely to be attacked. Also, you can install suction cup window shades on your side windows, and pull these down when you drive. They are cheaper, but they limit your vision.

Since long guns are difficult to hide in a vehicle, you will probably be taking incoming fire from a pistol. Consider whether or not you want to fire back. If you drive alone, a running fire fight is liable to detract from your good driving record.

Many years ago, I was asked to solve a similar problem for someone in high visibility who was afraid of being kidnapped. For $20.--, I went to a swap meet and brought an old single barrel shotgun with a broken stock. It's less than a two hour job to tape or wire this to a 2X4 and attach it to the underside of your car. One wire attaches to the shotgun's hammer, and the other to the trigger, and both run up around a pulley into the floorboard near the seat.

Load #2 shot. The critical item to decide is whether you want the weapon to aim to the rear or front. If it shoots to the rear, you can aim it so that, at 20 yards, the shot will move along the ground at radiator height. Problem is, if you don't take out tires and/or driver, the chase will continue for awhile. If you aim towards the front, the target is less vulnerable. A bumper behind most gas tanks, a rear seat behind passengers, and a badly angled rear window make a shot to the front relatively harmless.

Aiming to the rear, tires would be your best target. Aim your barrel slightly down and to the right so that jagged ricochets blow out front and rear right tires at the same time. Of course, at sixty MPH plus, the resulting fender-bender might ruin their whole day.

## RECAPS

We've designed one other invention to keep your homestead free of marauders. It will also do an excellent job out at sea.

Recaps is an acronym meaning REmote Controlled AirPlane. You can build them now so that carry a four pound payload, and you can fly them by radio control into anything. With an electric blasting cap and a couple of batteries, the circuit in the nose of the aircraft closes upon contact. Depending on the main explosive, you should get quite a bang out of it. You can deliver shaped charges, bottles of gasoline, etc to any target you can see.

Bigger and better recap's are being built. One bright medical doctor (Tamura), who invents things as a hobby, has figured out a way to double the lift on any wing surface by pumping high velocity air over the top. That will double the payload, thus giving you freedom to get exotic with a weightier explosive charge or fire starter.

I wish all of us would go go back to Biblical principles and live in peace. However, it doesn't appear that things will go that way. The news is worse daily. If things continue to worsen, put what you have learned here to good use and stay alive and unharmed.

## ANSWERS TO QUESTIONS FROM CHAPTER BEGINNING

a. Because you open the range, from which you can score, but he can't reach you. Get out to 300 yards, and play pepper---from a secure game standpoint.

b. No way! The best you can do might be 150 yards; and if he is fair, he can hit from 300 or better. If you must, close the range, but be mighty careful on the way in.

c. Take good cover and wait for him to move in. Don't expose anything. Try and figure out what load he is shooting, because the load is the critical factor in barricade penetration. Listen carefully so you know when and where he is moving.

d. Leave through a window, move into a well covered position at a good range away, and wait for the intruder to become an ex-intruder.

As soon as lights come on in your house, you can see in but they can't see out.

# Chapter 3

If you lose your guns...
## HOW TO MAKE AND USE
## HANDMADE WEAPONS

Like any material object, firearms and ammunition can be lost to a thief, a flood, earthquake, or atomic attack. So you could find yourself in a survival situation without firepower. No big deal.

A few people I know don't believe in warehousing firearms and ammunition. They figure, "If things get real tough and we get invaded, we'll just take some from the invading army."

Before an opportunity to acquire other firearms arises again, though, your own handmade weapons can mean the difference between life and death.

As you learned in Volume I, <u>Hand-to-hand Combat</u>, "Any weapon is better than no weapon.
What is a weapon? A weapon is:

ANYTHING THAT LENGTHENS OR STRENGTHENS YOUR SPHERE OF DEFENSE.

43

The definition is important, because it develops your thinking about combat.

How you think about your chosen weapon is just as important as knowing and understanding the definition. Any weapon you use must be:

## AN EXTENSION OF YOURSELF

The concept of a weapon being an extension of yourself says this:  The two of you must become one in action.  Don't make a weapon you can't use effectively in combat.  As we discussed in <u>Choosing Firearms</u>, you and the weapon have to marry up and work together.  If you can't handle it, either because you don't know how or because you're too weak, don't even spend the time carving it.

Finally, the weapon you choose to make has to match your ability to control it positively.  If you cannot maintain,

### POSITIVE CONTROL,

you would be better of with nothing, because losing a weapon changes things severely---you lose your big advantage, and your enemy gains it.

In Book I, we talked about the all- important concepts of hand-to-hand combat.  The same concepts also apply to handmade weapons.

Probably no concept is more important in its application than that of range.  If I can hit you with a big stick, you can't get close enough to strike me with a smaller one.  Because range is so important, we classify handmade weapons that way.

Also, any weapon you make will have to be constructed of materials that are readily available. When we combine range and materials, we develop this list:

SHORT RANGE
The Yiwara Stick
Knife

MEDIUM RANGE
The Baton
The Side-handled Baton
Sword

MEDIUM LONG RANGE
The Bo
The Spear

LONG RANGE
Bows and Arrows
Slingshots

We could have made a more extensive list, of course. But quantity means nothing. You need quality, both in fabrication and in user-ability. So we stuck to the weapons that were relatively easy to make and use.

As you did in firearms selection, examine yourself with an unbiased eye. Where is your strength? Arms? Lats? Legs? Do you have any severe weakness? You need to build your whole concept of handmade weaponry around your ability. Once you choose, make the weapon and practice with it.

Remember, "Get there fustus with the mostus?" If you choose a weapon that is like a sledge hammer, you will take a half dozen fists before you can strike once with it. Stay with what you know you can handle with speed and efficiency.

Most weapons increase the striking power of a blow many times over that which you could deliver on your own because:

A. They reduce the area of contact (while maintaining the same force) thus creating more target penetration, or,

B. Mechanically, they increase the velocity of the blow, and add the weapon's weight so that inertia carries through, into the target.

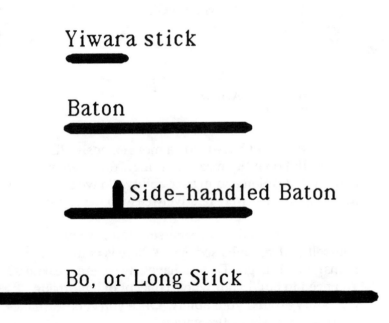

Four easy-to-make weapons. From top to bottom, the effective range increases.

## SHORT-RANGE CONFLICTS

Short-range conflicts can often be won because of a simple Yiwara stick. Basically, it's a short stick that you roll into your fist, and it sticks out on each end. Hawaiian law prohibits the use of Mace, so this is a great weapon for an island girl. It fits into a purse easily, and often doubles as a key ring.

How does it work? The force of any blow delivered is precisely measurable. It's the smack, or clout, of the blow (weight X speed), DIVIDED BY THE BLOW'S CONTACT AREA. So, given the same speed, I hit you with a softball, and then a golf ball, you can be sure that the last blow will do the most damage.

Say the stick represents one eighth of the area of my fist. A blow with the stick will increase the force received by a factor of eight times.

That's what the Yiwara stick does so well. Even so, there are problems: Hammer fist strikes take time to deliver, leave you open on the back swing, telegraph their arrival, and are easily blocked. You will have several opportunities for straight punches long before you can get a hammer fist shot.

Even so, I like the stick. Why? You can punch with it, and then reverse out, or cup in to double strike. The stick strikes in the other direction, that is, with the thumb side of the fist on an inside-out move. You are secure in punching, too, because it will keeps you from breaking a metacarpel, as I have done in Karate.

My own Yiwara is modified. I have drilled it and attached a key ring with a dozen keys. The keys are ground so that a sweep across someone's face will slice 'n dice. Whether you use the stick as a key ring or plain, it gives you an effective extra edge over the empty hand.

Almost all hand made striking weapons should be made from hardwood, and the Yiwara is no exception. Maple or Oak from the mainland, and Koa or Guava from Hawaii will work just fine. Of course, don't make any weapons from woods that split easily, such as Alder.

Making one is simple. The stick can be carved with a pocket knife. Make it fit your fist with at least your middle finger touching your palm when tightly closed--about as thick as a roll of pennies. More critical than thickness is length. It should stick out about an inch beyond each side of your fist. On the protruding ends, shape the point for penetration---the sharper the point, the more penetration into the target body.

In summary, this weapon's main function is to jab, either into the side of your target, down from the top, or up from the bottom.

After making one, practice your best strokes, then work on these motions while using resistence weights. In no time, you will develop strength, which when combined with this weapon, will turn you into a real combat threat.

In my opinion, a knife is more of a tool than a weapon. It is effective as a weapon, however, because it represents the ultimate reduction in surface contact area to the target. Thus the force is multiplied tens of times. For the same reason, it penetrates the body and destroys vital organs. Therefore, it's considered lethal.

Of course, we are talking life or death. It takes a long time for one man to acquire a killing mentality. If you haven't yet reached that degree of abject depravity, leave knives alone. I know of more than one person who only meant to scare somebody with a knife, so he cut with it rather than stabbed, but the psychogenic shock induced by the bleeding killed the victim. Knife killers normally go to jail.

Others who have used knives only as a scare tactic are dead. Why? Because the other guy took him to be dead serious and was trained. Several long range weapons as well as dozens of empty handed (Karate-Do) techniques make a knife worse than useless in the hands of an untrained, make- pretend knife-fighter.

We talk about the knife because it can be a short range weapon. If you decide to make one, however, think of it more as a tool. It carves points on sticks, bores holes in wood for traps, and attaches to a pole to make a spear. It also will help you zip through the woods like a pro, as we covered in Book III.

Obsidian (a flint-like rock) makes a super sharp cutting instrument. Simply use another blunt rock to produce the edge. You lay the knife edge down at approx. 45 degree angle, and push hard about a quarter of an inch above the edge to chip off several successive pieces. Turn the blade back and forth as you do this. Not only do you produce a sharp edge as the pieces break off, but it will be serrated. Don't worry about making it pointed. Other pointed weapons made from wood or animal horns are better for stabbing.

Chip away on the handle to slenderize it, and cover it with bark, wood, or cloth.

**

## MEDIUM RANGE

Let's mention the sword first. It's a long knife, so you can go offensive from a longer range. You don't have to get close to your enemy in order to inflict injury.

I don't like swords for the same reason I don't like knives. A long knife can be useful in a jungle or rain forest, but you will have to make it heavy, which means it will be unwieldy as a weapon.

You make a long knife the same way you make a short knife. Obsidian breaks easily, however, so any metal you can get your hands on will do better. With the flint stone approach, push down gently against the knife-edge to chip away quarter inch pieces until you have the blade reasonably sharp. Just leave enough handle for two hands.

The baton isn't anything more than a straight stick, somewhat rounded to improve grip, and therefore, control. Most modern law enforcement agencies have replaced the baton with the side-handled baton, a far superior weapon. But a straight baton is easy to make, and you may find yourself in a situation where time is a factor.

Batons are poor seconds to side-handled batons because:

A. It's difficult to wield properly without hurting your own wrist, so you seldom achieve good striking speed, and,

B. It's too easy to lose positive control over a baton during a one handed strike; therefore, you COULD lose it.

Once again, use hard wood. Not Alder. During a husband/wife domestic war in San Diego, a police partner of mine once struck a 240 pound customer over the head--only to shatter his baton. The customer continued to charge, and after a tremendous scuffle, we subdued him. The score: One police baton, broken beyond repair, rendered useless when needed most...history.

One customer cranium, seventeen stiches and blood loss, with severe headache, cured/healed.

The winner: Cranium--by a hard-headed decision.

The moral of the story: Any baton made with weak wood will shatter easily when it hits something hard, such as a forehead.

It's not hard to get good with a baton; just remember always to hold on with two hands. It is best employed as a jabbing weapon rather than a striking one. My favorite shot is a two-handed reverse circle that swings clockwise and ends up forcefully poking into the customer's abdomen. Still, it takes two hands..

You're a lot better off to cut a side-handled baton right out of a tree and scorch it over a fire. Not only will the wood be harder after a good baking, but you rub off the charcoal to shape it easier and better.

**Cut tree branch becomes Tonfa handle.**

**Try to find one perpendicular to main shaft.**

**Point both tonfa ends for great penetration**

THE SIDE-HANDLED BATON can be adequately maneuvered with only one hand; it's much better than the old, straight stick. It's called a TONFA by martial artists, and it turns you into a tank.

I bought my own from the Los Angeles Police Department, and it's made out of heavy duty aluminum. Ultra-superb. In training, the LAPD has beaten up on 2X4 lumber studs and shattered them. That's not all they break. If you swing hard and extend your swinging arm, the force stays with you. It comes back, and policemen who forgot to lift their left arm (right handers) out of the way, broke their upper arm. The've measured the force this weapon puts out on a lateral swing and it is TEN TIMES the amount of striking force obtained with other weapons. Awesome.

Here's the plan: Make a baton out of sturdy hardwood. Measure the bottom of your arm from closed fist to elbow; add five inches to overall length. Cut 'n carve. With the baton sticking out ahead of your fist by three inches and laid along your forearm, semi-close your fist, and locate a point on the baton under the crease across your palm.

That's where the side handle will attach. Side handle length will be the width of your fist, plus the thickness of the baton, plus one inch. Cut 'n carve the handle. Join the two pieces. If you don't have a drill, go the "Lincoln Log" route and notch the baton to accept a forked end on the handle. Then glue 'n screw.

## HOMADE TONFA

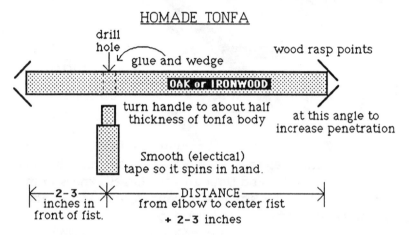

drill hole

glue and wedge

wood rasp points

OAK or IRONWOOD

turn handle to about half thickness of tonfa body

at this angle to increase penetration

Smooth (electical) tape so it spins in hand.

2-3 inches in front of fist.

DISTANCE from elbow to center fist
+ 2-3 inches

With any kind of karate training at all, this weapon is one of the best you can make, surpassed perhaps, only by the bo.

Here are a couple of my favorite moves:

**Reverse punch push**

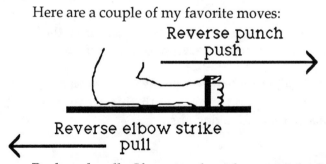

**Reverse elbow strike pull**

Push and pull. If you push with your right fist, as if to punch, and pull with your left, you will over-extend into your targets body. The baton moves forward and penetrates your target by a few inches and you will see the opponent in front of you go down.

Now, pull back with your right and punch out with your left; the baton will penetrate any target to your rear by a few inches, (because it sticks out behind your elbow). The guy behind you will probably drop as well.

Striking force multiplied 10 x's !

Arc of swing from right to left.

Arc swing (if you're right handed) from your right to left. Step in close, block up (raising arm block) and swing across and through your target's knees from the side. End this strike with your closed hand on the side handle hitting your left rib cage for safety. If you hit anything, the fight's over.. unless you didn't get close enough. In that event, keep your left arm raised, and backhand (for tennis players) as you step closer. That should do it.

Several good books have been written about TONFA, the best of which is named after the weapon itself, and written by Jarvis and Markloff.

As I said before, however, you're well off to learn one or two good moves with this weapon and then practice them for a day or so.

# MEDIUM LONG RANGE
## The Bo. The Spear.

I like a spear better than a knife or sword. Range is great because I don't have to get close. Essentially, it's a Bo with a sharpened point. The point can be a knife, a sharpened deer horn, or even the end of the shaft itself.

With green wood, you merely sharpen the tip and then cook it off over hot coals to harden it.

The problem with a spear is the temptation to throw it, and violate the positive control maxim. You spend all this time and effort making it, then throw it, miss, and your target carries it back to you--get the point?

spear

Of all the weapons you can make, the Bo is my favorite. It is positively controlled, easy to make, and devastating. Given minimum time and training, this is the first weapon I would make.

With a good hook on one end of the Bo, you can use it in the butt-stroke mode to foot-sweep an opponent down, or spear hook in from an undefended side. Of course, the rear end of the Bo, next to the hook, sticks out and can be sharpened down to any desired point size. The sharper the point, the more penetration into a target body.

**Bo from major tree limb**

cut tree branch

**Resulting hook on Bo provides excellent foot sweeper**

You hold the bo with two hands spread comfortably apart in the port arms position, and thereby make sure you have a good grip. The forward end is used for jabbing, and should be pointed to suit your penetrating style. I have also shaped a couple of mine with triangle or square edges on one end to get more penetration on a side strike, but shaped like this, the bo bruises my arm when I reverse it and snap down.

Each end of my Bo is pointed, although not severely. I shaped them just enough to get good penetration on a pool-cue shot to the foot. If you jab and break a metatarsal bone, your opponent will have to continue the conflict from the sitting position.

# LONG-RANGE WEAPONS

Bows and arrows, slingshots and traps produce enemy injury from a safe distance. That's the good news.

The bad news is: Once the weapon or projectile leaves your hands, you have zero control. You gave away your position, and if you did not score, your target will respond, often with more of an attack than you ever dreamed of.

Arrows need to be perfectly straight for accuracy, and the feather edges all must be exactly the same distance away from the shaft. Bows can be made out of any resiliant hardwood, and glue- laminated into a recurve. I like a bow and arrow and have hunted with both recurves and compounds for years, but you may not have the ton of time it takes to make one and master its use.

Slingshots are fine. David blew Goliath away with one. In my un-theological opinion, though, I don't think it was a fair fight; God helped.

Make a modern slingshot with the best surgical rubber and a quarter inch steel ball, so you develop a little over 200 feet per second. That will kill birds and rabbits, but only make a human target mad unless you hit a vital area.

You can bet a little more velocity with a swinging kind of slingshot, but you have to use perfectly smooth ammo for accuracy, otherwise, your shot curves. That's probably why David went to the river to choose smooth, round stones.

Several other handmade weapons can be useful. But trying to become an expert with many will leave you far behind somebody who SPECIALIZES with one. I watched Bruce Lee once and decided to become a Nung-chuk pro. I hit myself in the mouth. In the time it would take me to master this great movie-prop, I could learn to maim with something simple. You can too.

Once you learn to make and use the weapons listed here, you'll be combat efficient in most survival situations. You will have striking power way beyond the very Sunday-whallop best you could ever do with your bare hands, and that will give you the ability to conquer in most encounters.

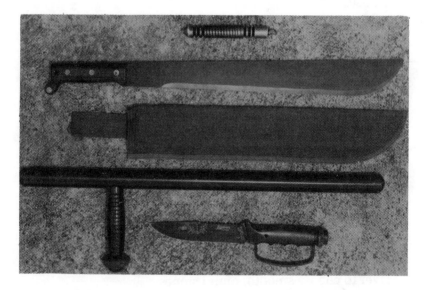

# Chapter 4

## GETTING AROUND IN GRUBBY TIMES

We benefit a lot and make progress because of interchanges with other specialists in society. They provide goods and a variety of services. If we couldn't travel, a lot of this interchange would stop. So, getting around is a good idea.

Even in grubby times, transportation will be important. Thus, you need to know about a number of alternate methods to get where you have to go.

To make sense of it all, let's examine transport in light of fuel availability.

| Using: | Travelling: |
|--------|-------------|
| FUEL | LAND |
| on | |
| NO FUEL | SEA |

In the beginning of any crisis, fuel will most likely still be available, in which event, a truck or van will be a great survival vehicle.

59

I like King Cab trucks because they carry six passengers, and they provide security for my gear. I also prefer a fleetside bed because it carries more.

A lot of people put great stock in four wheel drives. I don't, and I have owned several. Four wheelers drive your vehicle with two drive wheels, one forward and one back. So 4X4 really means two wheels driving. You obtain just about the same result with a positraction rear end on any truck. Posi's don't cost as much to buy or maintain and are not as heavy.

Whether you go with a truck, car, jeep, or van, modify it. Your local junk yard is full of all kinds of goodies and gadgets you can install on your truck or boat. Collect spare belts, bulbs and seal beams. Find a Mercury Montego (76, or so) and strip out a dome light, with duel aviation type reading lights attached. These are especially important if your vehicle is a van, and you sleep in it. Also, mount those lights on the outside. That way, you can light up your surroundings with a flick of a switch. Also, find an old pair of fog lights, and, perhaps, a spotlight.

If you won't be buying an expensive power winch, use a 12' chain hooked to your (horizontal) bumper jack. Also, rope or cable wrapped around an aluminum drum bolted on the lugs of your rear wheels will pull you out of just about anything.

Try and find a good trailer hitch. Install either a set of rails for the sides of the bed, or rope hooks. Add a second battery and bolt down a flat toolbox under the hood. Carry a spare alternator.

At a swap meet or any discount auto parts, you can find a variety of useful goodies to install in the cab. You need a CB radio and toggle switches. Add a fan if you operate in the desert or tropics. Cancel out the push button dome light switch on the driver's side so you can open the door unanounced at night. Rear window rifle racks advertise, and they don't give quick enough access. Seat covers with a built in gun case (under the knees) are widely available. I like stand-up gun racks too, but these are harder to find.

Forget radial tires. Once a sharp rock tears into the side of one, they can't be repaired. Go with 6-ply truck tires; you need lots of rubber between you and the ground. Mud treads are best, because road tires don't give you enough off-road traction. Rig your truck to carry two spares; off road rocks tear up rubber.

Wrap a cover over the steering wheel to keep your hands from burning (or freezing). Smoke or screen the windows. Put a hammock hook on the outside of the cab. Use a tree, (not coconut) or a fence post for the other end of the hammock.

I prefer the life style of a duck. I fly South for the winter and North for the summer. That way, I always sleep in warm weather. I also like sleeping near lakes and ponds because the water very often provides choice cuisine in the form of frogs, fish or waterfowl. Recreational swimming and bathing is also a great idea. But, near water, one insect can ruin your whole night.

You hit the sack really tired and just as you start to doze off, you hear a whine in your ear. You either have to roll up all your windows and suffocate, or, spend half the night slapping yourself in the face. Blood suckin'---disease carryin' mosquitos.

Sleep to the west of or under a large tree, and your van will stay cooler in the morning. Open the air vents in the driving compartment. As soon as the vehicle is sealed, light a candle. (MAKE SURE IT'S SECURE; YOU CAN'T AFFORD TO HAVE IT TIP OVER!) The little buggers will be attracted to the light, fly to it, singe their wings---and crash.

The preparation method is better. Buy a roll of screen and cut to fit. You keep the screens rolled up inside a carboard tube behind the seat. Use velcro fasteners. One thin line goes on the top of your roll-down window. The other goes on the top, just under the rain gutter. At night, attach the screen, and lower the side window just enough to stretch the screen tight.

Incidentally, security may be a problem; bandits often work parked vehicles at night. The solution: Bring a package of hot dogs to your local SPCA. That's the Society for the Prevention of Cruelty to Animals. A big dog that is very territorial will first bark and snarl at you. But if you can get it to take food from you and wag its tail, you may have a winner. Ask the Society for a chance to take the dog for a walk; spend some time with it. Just know this: If it barked and snarled at you, it will do the same to anyone else when it is chained to a van you are sleeping in. You get a full time security service for the price of dog food and love.

If you're like me, and you would like a bath after sleeping in your van in the Southwest, pull into just about any motel between sunrise and ten A.M. and let a maid read this:

** "Yo quisiera banarme.  Es possible que puedo pagar a Usted dinero para usar un quarto que no esta limpiada todavia?"

If you are even cheaper than I am, don't bother to ask.  The vacated rooms in a motel either have the key in the door, or the door is left open.  I feel more secure with the two dollar deal, however, so talk to the maid and pay her.  The Spanish translation:  **"I want to bathe myself.  Is it possible that I could pay to you money for to use a room that no is clean yet?"

Think about a covered utility trailer, to attach to your hitch.  It will store an immense amount of goodies, and a decent (one entrance) door will make security easy. (Lock and dog.)

Paint your survival vehicles.  Earl Scheib painted mine in Desert Sand, after which I sanded and primered various spots in Olive Drab.  Finally, I cut patterns out of folded newspaper, and painted a flat camouflaged color over the hole.  Result:  In the woods, my truck is difficult to spot.

Consider bullet-proofing.  Unscrew the door panels and install a layer or two of Kevlar; it will stop most small caliber bullets.

I have never been a motorcycle man, but they get great gas mileage, and they are cheaper to haul and store.  Make one mistake, though, and the medical bills will cost a lot more than savings on storage and gas.  If you read Book I of this series, you will learn in hand-to-hand combat that you never enter into battle unless the chances of winning are vastly in your favor. Motorcycle riders take on bigger cars and trucks daily, and lose---big time.

## IN A NO-FUEL SITUATION

Horses, mules, and llamas can be prized possessions. Your posterior may get a little sore riding them, but it certainly is better than carrying everything on your back.

Breed a female horse with a donkey, and you get a mule. They are sure footed, and a bit resistant to teaching, but well worth while. They don't get sick easily and are therefore reliable.

Llamas are increasingly popular. They are small camels without humps which can live on very little water. I interviewed a lady in Corvallis, Oregon who raises them and runs pack trips into Eastern Oregon. These are super sure-footed animals that can carry a 100 lb load for a long time. They feed on different kinds of leaves and lichens found in high mountains, so, unlike a horse, you big money isn't required to feed them.

The first time I hunted off horseback, I loved both the hunt and the horse. These animals are wonderful friends and workers. They are skittish because of an innate fear of snakes and bears, but you can use that fact to your advantage. Before you go to sleep, tie their halter to a tin can full of rocks and they will jerk it up to sound the alarm if danger approaches.

You and a horse can team up to do some great things. Since horses don't scare deer and elk, you can move in a lot closer than you could on foot. Of course, they pack a lot more, and carry you farther than you could ever go with your own two feet.

# FIREARMS FOR THE EQUESTRIAN

It's a good idea to carry a potent sidearm if you ride. When in danger, horses sometimes throw their riders, then run for it. Result, you're either left to face the danger (grizzly bear) alone, or, with your foot through a stirrup, the horse will drag you at a gallop. Remedy: Draw, and shoot.

A rifle carries nicely along side your saddle, and you can roll up a short shotgun in a bed roll or sleeping bag just behind your rump. For right handers, place it butt right if you plan on shooting off the horse's back.

## BACKPACKING

When all other transportation fails, you pack everything you own on your back and take it with you, wherever you walk. If you're financially embarrassed, they call you a bag man---one of the homeless. If you're rich, they call you a backpacker.

I have done this for years. Even if I stay at the Hilton, I take my rucksack. Why? Because it is easy to carry. ("Look, ma, no hands!") It contains your gear in easy-to-reach compartments; you can get what you need in a hurry. In Fiji, recently, I stayed at a very expensive hotel, and used a knife from my rucksack to prepare breakfast coconut. I could have used my hammock and netting to sleep outdoors. Inside the main compartment of my pack is a small, day pack. If I camp, I cache my main rucksack and take just enough for a day's hike 'n hunt.

Of course, I don't carry everything on MY own back. My dog carries a healthy load if we go on foot. He's responsible for carrying all of his own food, and quite a bit of mine. A few companies make kits for doggie-packs, but you're better off to tailor one to fit your own dog. Make the pack compartments detachable so that you can lighten the dog's load for day treks out of your base camp.

If you plan on a long trek, and you have maps available, pre-analyze the terrain so the trip won't be so tough. (See terrain analysis in the GREEN BERET'S COMPASS COURSE.) For any long hike, bring lightweight foods, which almost always means dehydrated. Nuts and seeds, plus dried fruits and vegetables, along with rice and chia seed should keep you fit and free of hunger. Marksmanship and backpacking are thought of to be individual skills. But survival backpacking (just like team shooting) is different; you go as a team. So commonly used items are distributed, one per hiker, and you share.

If you choose to live in snow country, learn to cross country ski and/or walk on snowshoes. Otherwise, think about a mountain bike, especially if trails and forest roads abound in your area.

## WATER TRAVEL

No matter where you go, plentiful water will be the key ingredient to successful survival. You'll use it for drinking, washing, toilet sanitation, and for putting out fires. In addition, water supports vegetation, which feeds a whole host of animals, both wild and domestic, which, in turn, feed man.

Moreover, if you live near a river or lake, you can use water for transportation by boat, raft or canoe. Boats come in basically three flavors: paddle, sail and power. Paddles work when all else fails; therefore, always take a pair with you.

Rubber inflatables go anywhere, and can be air-dropped easily. For a dive platform, they are easy to use, and you can swim with them out to your favorite coral spot, then anchor them and put your catch aboard, out of the water where a shark won't get the scent. (In southern USA fresh water, fresh fish loose in the bottom of the boat will attract snakes...)

My aluminum cartop boat fits on a rack I had installed on my utility trailer. I use an 18 horse outboard engine, and I can go into any body of water that I can drive near. Also, cartop boats are more stable than canoes and carry a bigger load as well.

You can jazz up your boat with stuff out of a junkyard just as you can a truck or car. Paint your boat camouflage too. Thieves can't steal what they can't see. An important thing on any boat is to build a place to keep everything out of your way. Paddles, gas cans, radios, batteries, guns and ammo should all have their own storage place.

Plastic milk cartons with foam filling make great floaters; tie these to your weapons for easy retrieval if you capsize. Insure your clothes and sleeping bags against sinking by packing them in water proof food containers, tied to the boat. In rapids, tie your fanny in too. If you carry a pistol on a belt with ammo loops, wear a surplus blow-up (B-12) life jacket. It's not a good idea to fall in the water wearing five pounds of gunbelt.

You can learn to sail rather cheaply, and a small boat costs about as much as a second hand car. To take advantage of one, however, you need to live in a place (like Hawaii) with good wind.

If you think you will be living without fuel, and you have access to reasonably calm water, stick with paddle power. A canoe is your best bet. They glide through the water with a lot less effort than other vessels and carry a good payload. When you paddle off one side, you have a tendency to move the bow to the other. Avoid this; keep your canoe on course with a "J" stroke. Feather your paddle out of the water sideways to stay quiet. Length is important---a seventeen footer carries a good payload. Since all animals come to water, lake hunting from a long canoe often pays off. Use binoculars to inspect the fine details on the water's edge. Canoes don't spook game much; don't stand up to shoot.

If you want more stability on your canoe, tie on an outrigger such as the one illustrated in EVERYBODY'S KNIFE BIBLE (From Pathfinder, $9.95). Outriggers are like training wheels on a kid's bike---they ARE a drag.

Now, it shouldn't matter whether you have fuel available or not. Whether it's by land or water, you'll be able to get where you're going, and carry a load with you.

*Where should you go when you got no place to go*
to...?

# Chapter 5

## RETREAT HABITAT

For human beings, habitat is a question of choice. We can live where we want, and God gives us an ability to adjust---to almost anything.

Some problems we just can't take. One is fear. Most people are good; a few are bound by rebellious compulsion to push the outer edges of the law. Since our criminal justice system doesn't work, and you can never tell who the bad guys are, I left the city and moved to the country.

If you are convinced that a survival plan is necessary, these are the choices:
1. Move
2. Stay where you are, or
3. Prepare a mobile facility, (truck or boat), and be ready to evacuate.

If #1, make sure to go where there is plenty of water, and figure out whether you want to live in a warm or cold climate.

If #2, then fortify and lay in supplies, or buy a survival retreat fairly close to home, and build that up.

If #3, install a good water filter on your mobile system, and improve/modify it so that it is secure, well provisioned, and ready for operation.

If moving will mean you will need new income, figure on learning a new way to support yourself. All kinds of books teach self sufficiency, and you can re-train yourself to do other labor.

Maybe you don't need a special place to go. It depends on where you live now, and what you think will happen in the future. If you live in Miami, LA, or San Francisco, you had better think about a survival retreat. If you are dependent upon a job now that will cease to exist after a crash, look for a different deal.

Often, it's possible to move twenty miles away and get enough rural seclusion to become almost totally self sufficient. If you are living from one paycheck to another and know that one unfortunate circumstance will leave you without food and water, face up to it; plan to leave. While times are still good, you can learn now how to tough it out. Our society is so strong that you could probably furnish your shack from junk piles, and welfare could catch you (for awhile) if you failed totally. But when times are tough for everybody, nobody will be able to help you.

In another chapter/volume, we'll teach you how to live off the land anyway, so money won't mean much. You'll be able to provide for yourself. You can raise livestock, grow food, and harvest from the land around you.

If you decide to move away from where you live, you'll be looking for a new, improved, survival retreat.

I moved from California to Oregon once and found that people are pretty much the same. I didn't see much difference between a California gang warlord and an Oregon lumber maggot. In California, it's hot rods and booze; in Oregon, it's souped up log trucks and beer. Same/same.

So, survival problems differ according to geography. For example, Oregon coastal mountain ranges enjoy 30 days of straight rain. Everything gets moldy. Then it gets cold. We survived by canning fruits and vegetables and cutting and drying about ten cords of firewood every summer. Electric blankets and comforters were great, as were warm clothes, boots, and waterproof coverings.

At another time, I lived in the desert west of Los Angeles. I didn't need much firewood. If I had waterproof gear, I would have turned it upside down and tried to catch a drink. A friend of mine, Wynn Williams, owned a junkyard; one day he went into a wrecked car to unbolt a part and ran into a rattlesnake! It scared the daylights out of him, until he realized the snake was dead---from heat prostration. "It was right then," he said, "that I knew I was working in too hot a climate." He moved to San Diego.

If you have no job, no family, no responsibilities, you can think foreign country, in which event, think about language, customs, people, crime, governmental stability, laws, weather, social life, church, and relative economics. I've thought about foreign countries---a lot. I speak several languages, and have a built-in capability for adapting. Even with all this, I am not too keen on them.

I wouldn't go to Mexico on a bet, and I speak the language fluently. The people are fine but the government is rotten. I used to transport food across the Tijuana border for starving orphans, and the Mexican border guards would steal a little "mordida."

71

But that was ten years ago, now, they're worse. Our DEA agent, Camarena, was beaten to death by Mexican Police officers who had been bought by drug dealers.

I thought the Phillipines might be excellent. Everything is cheap in this poverty stricken country. At this writing, secretaries who can type earn $2.00 per day. But the government there also is absolutely rotten. I talked to a young Air Force Sgt in whose car a police colonel planted marijauna, then tried to solicit a bribe. The Sgt left the country. Inside sources I knew told me the Marcos government wouldn't last another two years. How about Corazon? Better, but only at the top. You are still looking at a country infested with criminality at the lower governmental levels. Marcos installed people like himself. Of course, any president of a country that rips it off for 10 billion when the average income of an educated worker is $30 per week can't be all bad. The residue: theft, murder, and aids-infested prostitutes.

Korea did not look bad. It's an up and coming country following in Japan's developmental footsteps. Seoul stinks of smog, but the southland still has a lot of fresh air. I was impressed. I talked to an American there who makes $10 per hour teaching English, and $10 will buy four good polo shirts or a pair of excellent running shoes.

Reports from Canada indicate a general downhill slide, but it has tons of space in which to hide.

Australia and New Zealand all have plenty of room, but some anti-American sentiment abounds. I have talked to tourists from New Zealand at length, and they complain about the vast drain on New Zealand resources from South Pacific natives who qualify for welfare. I went there and travelled up and down the country. Loved it. Not many people live there, (3 million) and most of them are the finest kind. Food's cheap, and for 70 American cents they give you a dollar.

They have a minor Maori problem, but they are handling it. What I liked best was the land itself. Lots of fish, game, and timber. I probably will go back.

I spent quite a few months in Australia. I have travelled all over the world  and find the Aussies to be the finest anywhere. Big country. Almost the size of the US, with the total population of Los Angeles, so there is room. Sharks, poisonous snakes and spiders made it a bit scary, but the cities were nice. They are about ten years behind the US in many ways, so the crime and drug wave hasn't hit there yet.

Leave out Europe. It's too crowded and it's more than difficult to break into their society. The Danish countries are the best, but it's cold! Germany would be second, but it's also cold, and some of the people have become radical.

Guam is a beautiful Island. The elected govenor of the Island got out of our Army on a Section 8. He is in jail now, anyway. I spent a week there in early '85, and seven men had been raped during the first quarter. Shootings and stabbings are practically ignored. An Anderson Air Base cop told me Guam has the highest crime rate of any part of the U.S. Pass on Guam; too much crime and degeneracy.

Some South Pacific Islands look good to me, and I am investigating. I went to live in Fiji. Not bad. Cost of living is only high there if you live American. Food abounds, as does water. Recent politial trouble seems to be settling down. Rent $300 for classic house. Sleep under netting. Excellent diving. Many good and honest vilage people with big smiles. They put my computers in jail because I wouldn't pay the import tax, and when I left, they gave them back to me, no sweat. Try that in Mexico...

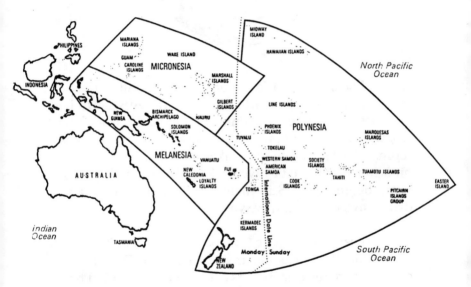

In our own Hawaiian Islands, there is plenty of room and water. The populated Island of Oahu contains 91% of the population but less than 10% of the land area. One Island gets 400 inches of rain per year; the rest get enough. I find most of the people friendly and full of the Aloha spirit. It is absolutely the friendliest place in which I ever drove my car. Some areas offer some anti-white sentiment, however, and a criminal element does exist. You can obtain a 60 minute cassette tape telling you all about Hawaii from Pathfinder Publications, 150 Hamakua #401, Kailua HI, 96734. Cost: $9.95, or $7.95 if you bought one of Pathfinder's Books. Pathfinder pays postage.

No matter where you go, you need plenty of water. You can go without food, but water is a must. It not only supports you, it supports a bunch of different animals you can eat. Water is the reason I love the Northwest and the Islands. They both have plenty. I can always drink freely, plus enjoy flourishing vegetation.

Once the water problem is solved, the next big question is: how far will your vehicle or boat range? If you live in Miami, don't think about moving to Oregon because, when things get tough, you won't have enough gas. Also, plan to steer clear of any populated area.

If you go by boat, you will be sailing. Read SAILING THE FARM, a great book about someone who sailed all over the world. Boats are cheapest to buy in Tahiti, because so many people make it that far and then become thoroughly fed up with it. Face it---sailing a boat is work, and that work is frequently done in an atmosphere of fear and stress. When you sail a boat, you must pay attention, and if you don't, you lose your boat, and perhaps your life. Screw up and the ocean doesn't forgive you easily; an aquaintance left his yacht ($92,000) on a Tahitian shoal.

On a sail boat, a solar still makes your fresh water, a food dryer takes care of staples, and you learn to eat fish. Each island becomes a giant fruit store, and coconuts and bananas are counted as blessings. With a solar food dryer on board, and a good supply of sealable plastic storage, your diet on a  long voyage will step up in class and variety.

One writer dipped his silver and gold in tar and left the pieces under the oil in his bilge. He travelled from island to island--not bad. In port he cut hair and tied net for a living, and he was successful enough to provision sufficiently for the next leg of his journey.

Probably you will get away from it all by auto/truck. Using your vehicle range (with extra gas additions) to determine mileage limits, draw concentric circles on a map from your home location, and start searching for a new place to reside. Within the circles, find first a place that offers water, then hunt for good topographical features that provide safety from the elements as well as intruders.

Boaters and land rovers learn different skills. Instead of hunting deer, we snorkel and shoot fish with a rubber-propelled pole spear. One summer I made my 12 & 14 year old daughters live in a tent in Hawaii (safe on a military reservation), and I spearfished for them. We did well. A dinner meal of bar-b-qued lobster and baked potatoes was followed by another featuring manini and palani. Then I shot a squid and the kids rebelled. They borrowed the car and went to Jack-in-the-box. A few days later, I drifted around the bottom, stuck my eyeballs too close to a coral hole and met a Moray eel head-on. I made the water warmer right away as I got out of there. Back to Jack's, but the whole experience was profitable.

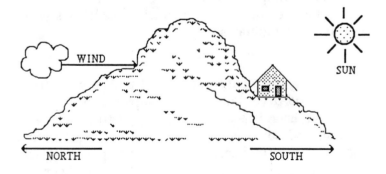

For land rovers, pick a site as you do in camping. Deep valleys won't work, and swamps are out. Your best bet is a hillside, where natural rains run off the property, and you have a command view of the terrain below. In Oregon, it rained over fifty inches a year, and once in a while the wind really blew hard, so a hillside was great. It took a minute or so for even a fast car to wind up our noisy gravel driveway, so we were always prepared. From the front of our lot, we could see down into a long valley below, and we clear-cut the whole four acres so we had a field of fire.

If you can't live without utilities, consider whether or not your intended retreat has them, and how stable they are. Plan on going without power for a few days every year during a storm. Oil lamps provide lighting. Cut firewood will heat your home, and water pressure should be from gravity. Electricity is nice, but you need strong wind or good water drop to generate it, unless you find a place that sunshine blesses, in which event, solar electric will work.

Pre-investigate the locale in which you intend to settle, and pre-plan the physical move. Hopefully you will have enjoyed numerous outings to the site, and you will know the surroundings like the back of your hand. Likewise, you should know several ways to get there. Chances are that when the flag does go down, several roads will be either closed or too dangerous to travel, and you will need to know about alternate travel routes, especially off-road.

Not only I, but Woodcroft (author, Book I) think convoys are best. Even sailing, we take more than one boat, if possible. The same principles found in the Green Beret team concept (Book I of this series) apply to travel; go with a variety of talent. The medic is there, and your tools and mechanic go along.

If you need specific information, you can send a scout with a radio to report back. That way the whole team avoids a roadblock or riot, but the whole team is also ready to saddle-up in the event you encounter trouble.

Even on a hunting trip, we travel by convoy. We practice on the radio. If it's clear to pass around a curve, the lead car gives the word. Hazards are announced over the airwaves. We also practice working as a team by co-ordinating; one vehicle carries our nutritionist who feeds the team during stops and breaks. Another has the medic, and a third carries construction and destruction gear, like chainsaws and explosives.

Once you arrive, you can take over quickly and set up, then establish some control of the surrounding area. All team members can begin operating in their specialties, and you will be safe and secure in your new retreat habitat.

"I bought my first chainsaw before they became real popular tools. Then, I started falling trees and carving furniture. After that, I moved to Oregon and learned from professional lumberjacks. There's old timber fallers, and bold timber fallers, but no old-bold timber fallers. Here's what I learned from an old one, one of the best".

--Don Paul

# Chapter 6

## HOW TO FALL BIG TREES

Your first step in using wood for anything is to drop the tree on the ground, so falling is basic. But it's dangerous; most accidents happen to fallers. When falling, the key trick is <u>GET IT DOWN SAFELY.</u>

If you kill a tree without knowing exactly how, the tree may get even as it hits the ground. If you don't care about safety, suture self...

Incidentally, you will need a few extra tools and accessories. Since you can't begin to fall a tree unless you know exactly where it leans, you need a plumb bob (a fishing sinker on a bright nylon string). Wedges (plural) are important.

The standard safety equipment is a good idea; a hard hat is a must, and ballistic nylon chaps keep those deep, crippling cuts out of your legs. Ropes and a come-a-long or winch, and, perhaps, a snatch block (pulley wheel) will also help. Once outfitted, you're ready to knock over a tree.

Most injuries occur because the faller forgot one little detail, so, for safety's sake, we developed a checklist. Copy this and carry it with you into the woods. Here's what to do:

### 1. ANALYZE THE AREA
Snags; hangers; widowmakers; weather conditions---wind! Terrain; choose a flat falling area.

### 2. ANALYZE THE TREE
Surrounding obstacles; walk the "lay." Check tree's lean and weight; bark composition. Saw hazards and tree health.

### 3. SWAMP OUT
Plenty of room; forty-five degrees to the rear; alternate escape route.

### 4. FACE CUT
Commonly too narrow; open for control. Cuts meet evenly. Final check: Square to falling line.

### 5. BACK CUT
Straight in; two inch stump shot; wedges in as soon as possible; matching holding wood for even pull.

### 6. ESCAPE!
Don't hesitate; leave saw if necessary. Go six yards and take cover.

Now let's see how to apply the checklist. The most frequent injuries occur because, as soon as the tree he was working on began to fall, the faller didn't run and hide behind a another tree.

The tree you drop can "barberchair," which means split up the middle and send the top half back to crush your body. Even if the tree falls correctly, it can scrape another, and send flying limbs all over the forest, some of which can spring back at you with power you wouldn't believe.

Flying wood comes from a variety of trees. For example, snags (dead trees that are still standing). Depending on how dead and rotten they are, they can keel over on you because of the vibration of another tree hitting the ground far away, or they can break in three pieces, and drop down in a 50 foot kill radius. Hangers are fallen trees that hang upon another tree, sometimes by only one branch. Anyone nearby is in danger, because when a hanger lets go, it usually throws branches and debris all over the general area.

Widowmakers are worse. These are loose, barely attached limbs high above the ground that are slightly supported by another tree's green, healthy limbs. You spot them by looking for limbs that go across others instead of out from the trunk, and you keep looking up while you are cutting so you can dodge any you might not have spotted. Obvious widowmaker hazards are best handled by falling another tree so it brushes the widowmaker to the ground.

If the wind is blowing, don't fall a tree. A little wind can send your tree over the wrong way, bringing havoc.

Swamp out an escape route. Before cutting any tree down, make sure you have a way to get out of there. Experts agree that the safest way to run is on a line forty-five degrees to the rear of your intended falling line. Swamp out in that direction by cutting back and forth with the saw, eliminating every possible obstacle. The wrong time to have your clothes snag on a twig is when a big tree limb is about to crush you.

Before you cut, you have to estimate the lean of the tree; find out which way it would fall if the roots vanished. Either use a weight on the end of a line or an ax, but hold it up in the air so it hangs plumb down, and compare the tree. Then walk a quarter of the way around the tree and take another look. If you have to fall the tree against it's natural lean, call a pro. Otherwise, put the tree down somewhere within a 180 degree arc, the middle of which is the direction the tree leans in. To do this, you will make a face cut on the compression side of the tree.

We refer to every tree, limb, or log as having a compression side and a tension side. To grasp the concept, bend a twig in front of you. On the outside radius of the curved twig, the wood fibers are in tension. On the inside, the fibers are in compression.

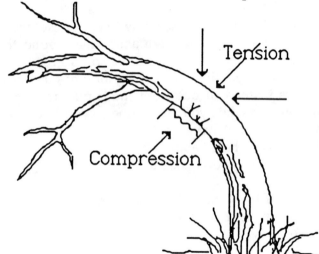

If a tree leans, the side closest to the ground is in compression. The other side is in tension. Limbs are the same. A log spanned across a gully is in tension on the bottom, compression on the top. Understanding this theory is a MUST, for it applies to all tree cutting situations.

The tree falls over because it leans over and compresses (where you put the face cut), and the tension is released when you backcut it.

You square the face cut by sighting down the "gun," which is a raised plastic line on the saw's body perpendicular to the cutting edges of the saw. If there is no gun on the side of the saw, sight down the handlebars; they, too, should be perpendicular to the bar edge.

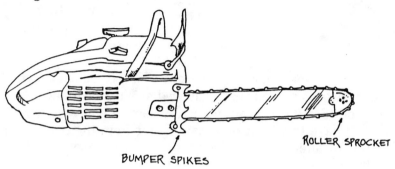

BUMPER SPIKES

ROLLER SPROCKET

In EVERYBODY'S KNIFE BIBLE, we teach you how to modify your knife so you could figure out exactly how high any tree is. This is hot information if you are working in a crowded area (like a town) and you don't want to demolish anybody's outhouse.

Now that the face is perfect, it's back cut time. Mentally draw a level line back from the point of the face-cut "V" to the other side of the tree. Raise the saw two inches above that point, and begin a level back cut (towards the face) making sure that the holding wood will be equally thick on both sides.

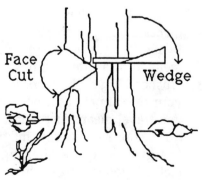

Face Cut

Wedge

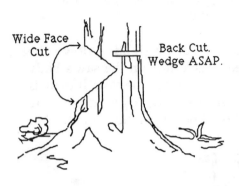

As soon as the bar is deep enough into the wood, chip away the bark with your ax and plant a plastic wedge in the back cut. Drive it in tight, then continue to cut. This is a necessary precaution because weight and lean are frequently misjudged.

Should that happen, tons of wood will sit down backwards on your bar. The wedge is bar insurance---a good idea if you want your saw back. Otherwise, you will have to unbolt your saw motor from the bar, and return later with another saw to cut yourself out of trouble.

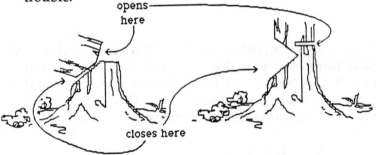

As the chain approaches the back cut, about two inches away, you should notice the top starting to move. BOOGIE! Hesitate and you might understand the feelings of a jilted high school girl after a prom---just crushed. If you have to, leave the saw. You run down your retreat path at least six yards, but every extra yard you travel means just that much more life insurance; so don't conserve energy, hustle---and take cover. When the ground quits shaking, go back and enjoy the feeling...you're king of the woods.

Next, trim the limbs. Carefully! Don't cut from the downhill side. A limb wedged into the ground may be the   log on hillside only thing holding the log   with jambed limb from rolling over your body.   holding it. Look things over before you cut, and pay close attention; you may have to move quickly.

Pay extra attention to the tip of your saw while cutting. If that tip touches a hidden limb at high chain speed, the saw will kick back on you.

If you want firewood, cut from the tip of a limb toward the trunk, alternately cutting down (pulling chain), then up (pushing chain), and dropping wood on each cut. Otherwise, shear off the limb close to the trunk.

After cutting the limbs, begin bucking the trunk. Always cut the compression side of the log first. If the log you are bucking is in a lot of compression, think about using a wedge to keep the kerf from closing in on your saw. Wedges are also needed on steep hillsides where the log lies up and down.

Remember this---no matter how good you are, or how much you've learned, bucking surprises are common. Always be ready to run for it. DON'T hang around and try to take the saw with you; your life isn't worth it.

Now that you know how to get the trees down and get them into pieces, here's how to make yourself comfortable.

With a saw and a few extra gadgets you can make a great place to live and furnish it like a palace.

I bought a campground full of oak trees just about the time I learned how to use my first saw. Some of the campground's old oak trees are now old oak furniture. I liked it so well I really got into design and

85

cutting. You can do the same; it's easy.

Chainsawn furniture will be virtually indestructible furniture, and last for ages. Just learn the principles and apply them to every piece you create. No matter what kind of wood, or how big the log, everything can be reduced to functional beauty; just sharpen your saw, lay out your work, and start carving.

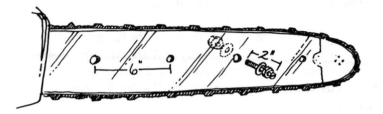

Begin by modifying the saw. Drill holes in your saw bar every six inches. Of course, add special holes for special depth. Then fasten a two inch screw through any hole with nuts and lockwashers on each side of the bar, and that will stop the bar from plunging too deep into a cut. Besides bar stops, you need a level, a snap line, and a large square. If you normally cut with chisel chain, switch to chipper (with the rounded corners) or buy a ripping chain.

Function controls design. Figure out how you spend your time and design furniture that will make your life more enjoyable.

With any normal bed, the space above is lost. We raised our bed and gained 35 sq feet of additional living space. Under that bed we built in dressers, closets, a desk, book shelves and other storage. We wired it for sound, also. The heat in our room is trapped near the ceiling, so we sleep warmer, and our smelly hound dog never climbs on our bed.

This is the first piece of home furniture I would build because it's easy, and because I spend time here, no matter what. I can live without a living room, but if I am going to function well in the woods at all, I have to sleep well.

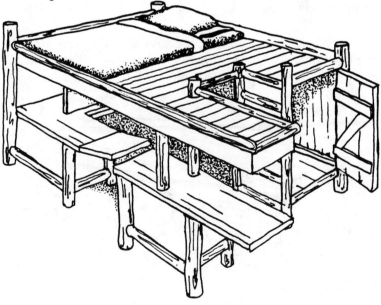

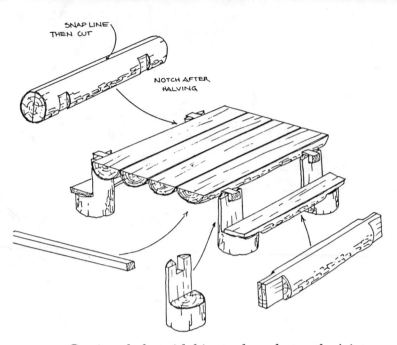

SNAP LINE
THEN CUT

NOTCH AFTER
HALVING

Carriage bolts with big washers fasten the joints. It's easy to make the camper's dream. Cut all the poles from the straight limbs off any tree. It takes down in minutes, and all the poles lay side by side in your pickup. The flat piece in the back is held by chain or rope, and can be used for desk, workbench, table, or counter top for the cook.

While we were at it, we invented the desk that can't be stolen. Or, if somebody does pick it up and carry it off, be very polite to them.

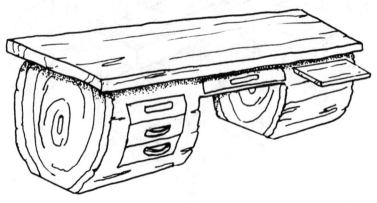

We started with a log. After flattenig the bottom, we held a level line at the seat and spray painted on top of newspaper wrapped over a straight edge. After boring into the log with the chainsaw, we merely cut on the bottom of the paint line to make nice seat.

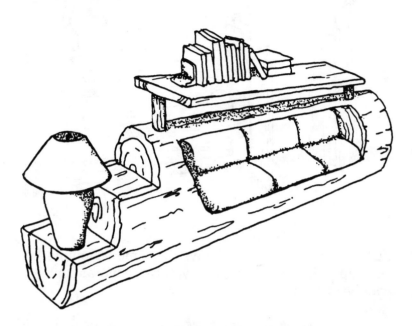

I like a removable desk top because the work angle can be adjusted. Also, it's a lot easier to bore cut from the top and cut out a cube, which is replaced with the drawer frame insert. Finally, it requires only that you move two separate short logs, rather than one big one. When you have them in postion, you set the top.

Even less portable is the living room couch. It looks complicated but can be cut in a few hours. Anytime you want to add shelving, you bore sideways into the log, then cut and trim a few oblong pieces from the limbs. I douse mine with glue and jam them in the slot with a sledge hammer.

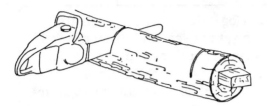

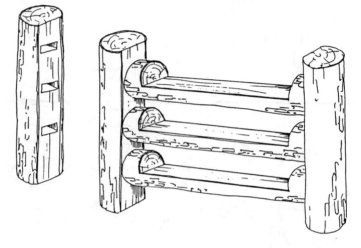

Let's talk about "how to." Almost all chainsaw furniture construction employs the same techniques; just apply the principles, and you can build anything your heart desires.

Debarking the whole piece is a good idea. The bark will eventually fall off anyway. My favorite debarking tool is a leaf from a car or truck spring. I tape on a good handle, and sharpen the other end on one side only, so it works like a chisel.

Since furniture should rest firmly on the floor, start by stabilizing.

If your floor is level, use one of two methods to level the bottom. The cheaper method is to drag the log behind your truck. Choose a newly paved street or a supermarket parking lot to let the asphalt rub it down until it's flat on the bottom. Once your log rests flat on the ground, you're ready to carve on it.

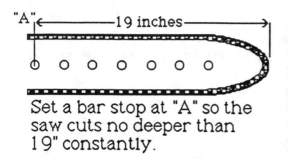

"A" |←———19 inches———→|

Set a bar stop at "A" so the saw cuts no deeper than 19" constantly.

If the piece is for seating, start by cutting the back of the seat. Roll the log slightly to the rear and prop it up with wedges on the bottom so that a round log with back cut 19" from floor to seat. Then show vertical (straight up and down) cut will create fifteen degrees of incline after the bottom is flat on the ground again. Set a stop on your bar so you sit down nineteen inches from the floor.

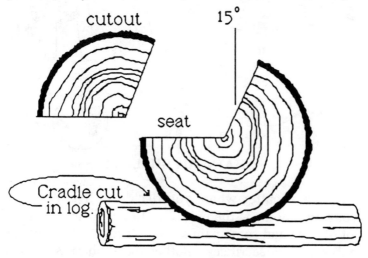

cutout        15°

seat

Cradle cut in log.

Once the back is finished, cut the seat. This has to be level, especially from left to right. Measure up from the ground on both ends of the proposed seat cut, and snap a line. Level a piece of cardboard and tack it on the front, the spray-paint (white) over that, so you have an easy, level line to follow as you cut out the seat.

After the cutout pops loose, the finish work begins. Smooth out the seat and back with a plane (power or hand) and then chisel the corners.

91

Most people stand in the middle of the woods and can't see the forest for the trees. Now, you can stand in the middle of the woods with a chainsaw, blink your eyes like a Genie, and know that you are standing in the middle of the world's largest furniture store--and it's all free...

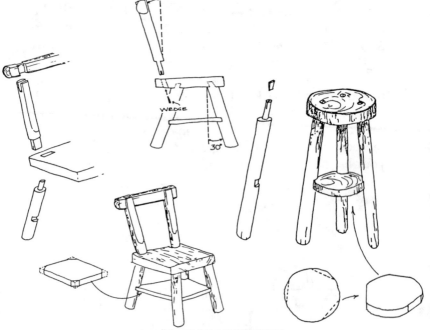

**CHAINSAW SHELTER**

No matter where you decide to live, building your own home is the only way to go. Even though a lot of time and some pain are involved, the benefits far outweigh the sacrifices. Rather than inherit someone else's ideas and ways of building, you can build a custom house (tailored to your needs), and it will be strong. Any home built with almost free timber will stand like a fortress compared to one built with costly sticks.

Long before thinking about what to build, consider where. Even before you draw one building line on paper, spend a lot of time selecting a site. Get high and dry and choose good foundation soil, not clay or shifting sand. In a poor location, no amount of extra reinforcement will do any good. You can't fight mother nature. Old river beds only work for houseboats.

What to build? The possibilites are endless. What you need to do is protect yourself from the elements. Normally, you use a chainsaw to build something heavy and substantial, which you will need in a cold, rugged climate. That's rough, because in that kind of weather, you have limited time during which to build (at least the shell). In the tropics, on the other hand, you have all year to build, and a minor shelter will suffice.

Translation: In an area where the climate is harsh, you will have to knock out the structure pretty quick. So your thinking has to change. Option #1: If you build a palace, either get a lot of help, or start small and add on later. Option #2: Build a mini-palace (Log Hex House) in a hurry; work like a slave.

Option #3: Build a quickie (Alaskan); get in out of the cold, and work on the mother structure as time and weather permit.

Log construction adapts to almost any house plan. In addition, add-ons are easy. Even if you cut into a roof-bearing wall for a new addition, large logs across the top of the opening will still support the roof.

The only real problem will be bureaurocracy. Recently, I moved to an area I thought would be far enough out in the country to escape "burro-cratic" stupidity. I developed the hex house. The whole structure was supported by a 34 ft. beam, 18"X12", which I cut and carved out of a standing tree. The county building inspector got involved, but couldn't figure it out. So he consulted with architectural professors at Oregon State U. Last I heard, they were still consulting.

Not only the hex-house, but the Alaskan is noteworthy. Both are easy and QUICK to build. Inside of a month, the roof will be finished and you'll be sheltered inside.

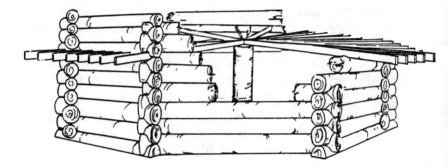

We discuss the hex- house first. It yields maximum footage from minimum labor, and approximates the heating efficiency of the geodesic dome. In hex house construction, all the walls are the same, so the walls + roof go up in a hurry. Once you're inside and cozy, you can take all the time you need with plumbing, electrical and interior partitions. A relatively new tool, called a "squangle" helps to figure out the odd, inside angles.

## ** LOG HEX HOUSE PLANS**

Draw a circle; the radius will be equal to one of the six sides. I used a sixteen foot radius and sides for my first attempt, which made the walls easy to handle and provided 670 square feet on each floor.

No matter what you build, a good foundation is helpful. Treated wood sunk into the ground will work for a long time, but someday it will be a bear to replace. Cement is probably best for every application. You make forms according to any kind of floor plan you intend to use, and pour concrete into them. If you can find cedar or redwood, use that on top of the cement; it won't dryrot.

In some areas, however, cement isn't available. Hauling precast pyramid blocks may work for remote areas. Set the blocks into wet Ready- crete sacks of pre-mixed cement-sand-gravel poured over a bed or rocks. The blocks don't have to be on the same level with one another, just level across their tops, (two ways). You merely post up from the blocks (cut to fit up to your support beam level), then lay the floor decking.

Once you have decided on a foundation, think about plumbing. Without a government water source (and you can't get water unless you have a building permit), you need to locate a spring, or dig a well. You need water coming into the home at several locations, and you need it coming out at no less than two places. Contrary to bureaucratic code, I plumb so that white water goes out in one place, and toilet water into another.

Generate your own electricity with a fuel powered generator (cheap), or a water powered unit, or wind power (costly). You may want to run some power in through the foundations, although I prefer to place the main electrical panel on an outside wall.

All six walls will be the same length, sixteen feet, so eighteen foot logs, (with a foot over on each end), will do nicely. We call the fat end of a log the butt end. Build the walls with the butt ends of the logs alternating--one thick end to the right, then one thin end, both on the same side of the wall.

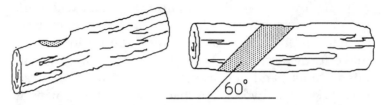

Cut a sixty degree channel in each log
to the curvature of the log it will fit over.
Then, flip the log; it'll fit like a glove.


For a hex-house, you need only one joint, and
that is a saddle notch sawed out at a sixty degree angle
which will be lapped over an intersecting log. The cut
out saddle fits over (NOT UNDER) the top of its
intersecting neighbor, so no rain gets into the bare
wood. That helps prohibit dry rot.

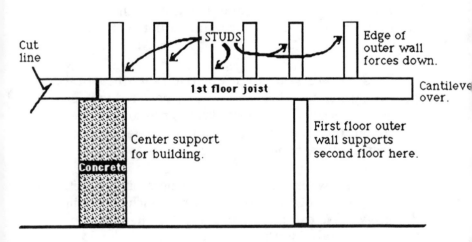

Cantilever the ceiling joists on the first floor and extend the second floor's walls outwards. This would provide you with much better view and shooting cantilever detail ND capability. (I shot a couple of deer from mine while I was typing upstairs.) If the bottom floor had only one barricaded door and you used high, clerestory windows, the place would be hard to burglarize.

The Hex-house uses a cathedral roof, which takes time because you need to build a temporary standing platform in the center of the building in order to bring the rafters together. When building out of logs, use rafters twice as long as you need them. That way, you can easily balance them across the walls, and maneuver them into place so someone can nail them at the apex. Leave them long, and cut in windows or skylights for natural lighting. You can always cut the rafter tails later. You also have the option of using u-bolts set in concrete to tie them down for extra stability.

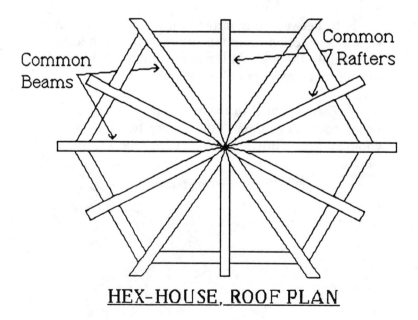

HEX-HOUSE, ROOF PLAN

The cathedral roof uses only six common beams from corners to the center. If you go with log construction, use a line level or a clear hose full of water to find equally high points on the ends of your walls. After you mark both ends of the top log, snap a chalk line on it and roll it ninety degrees; then dog it so it doesn't move, and chainsaw your line by holding the saw's bar up and down as you move along the log.

(TOP VIEW)

CATHEDRAL ROOF

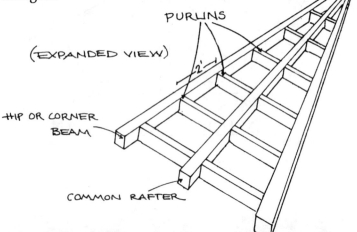

In between our rafter beams from each corner, we added another common rafter from the middle of each wall to the top. At the apex, horizontal collar ties prevent roof stress under heavy snow load.

Then, parallel to the walls, purlins bridge from corner beam to common rafter every two feet, and the whole roof structure then covers with solid sheating and shingles.

PURLINS

(EXPANDED VIEW)

HIP OR CORNER
BEAM

COMMON RAFTER

After the roof is on, cut out window holes. Simply buy the window, and cut a hole three inches bigger on every side. Then frame it by setting (vertical) trimmers and a window sill with lumber. We sealed our openings with cans of expanding foam, but moss or fiberglass also insulate fairly well.

## THE ALASKAN

You don't need to draw plans for this. You can build it as fast as you can draw it. When you need to be inside a structure fast because unbearable weather is trying to hurt you, this is the way to go. Wait till the stormy season passes; then, during a few months of nice weather, you can build a castle. The Alaskan will always be useable for storage or hurricane retreat later on.

This log end structure is strong, and it can be built with only the tools you'd probably have with you way out in the boondocks. Cordwood- wall construction is easier because you don't have to move heavy logs around. In a day or two, you can saw up a few cords of firewood, split the sides off and stack them to form a wall. Build it under ground or into the side of a hill, if possible, because earth is a super insulator. Digging, setting drains, and vapor-shielding will take some time also.

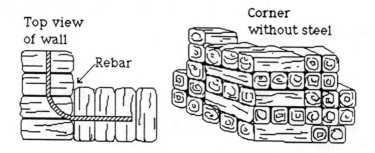

Top view of wall
Rebar
Corner without steel

Square off the round logs with a mall or a splitting wedge. With squared off sides laying against each other, you'll use less mortar, which saves time and money, and also gives the wall better insulation value.

Start by bucking up the nearest trees into log ends, say, a foot and a half long. Remember that wood has an R factor of one per inch, so an eighteen inch wood wall would insulate to R-18, and that's plenty, especially underground.

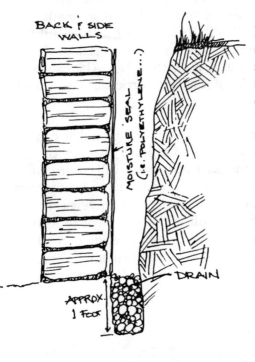

BACK & SIDE WALLS

MOISTURE SEAL (i.e. POLYETHYLENE...)

DRAIN

APPROX. 1 FOOT

(SMALL ROCKS, GRAVEL...)

Lay the log ends on top of one another and seal them with a mortar mix of cement, sand and lime. Tie corner intersections one of three ways: Nail strapping from one wall to another; bend rebar 90 degrees and extend it into corner mortar; or, without steel, cut a few logs a foot longer than others, and extend these into the intersecting and abutting wall.

If you build the back wall a foot higher than the earth, you can install a narrow window to provide light and a worms-eye view uphill. The side walls then have to angle down to the height of the front wall.

On the outside of the walls that are set into the ground, you will place a  moisture seal; heavy plastic sheeting is fine; don't puncture it with corners.  At the outside bottom of the moisture seal, set a plastic pipe with holes in the top half.  Lay screen over the holes, then back fill the three walls.

Now all you need is a front wall with a window and door.  If you build with mortar, you can't chainsaw a window or door hole in a wall.  So, you build the frames first  and lay up the cordwood (custom cut) against them.

You need level, horizontal lines across the front and rear walls, especially if you will shed roof and make the roof angle follow the ground contour.  Be exact. Cordwood walls are easy to build level, but you have to take the time and effort to get it right.  Otherwise, roofing will be a nightmare.

Start the roof.  For short spans, use a shed roof. (Flat roof angled low on one side). If you keep the angle of the shed roof the same as the hillside, you can grow grass on top.  That leaves only the shelter's front to camouflage and conceal.

You need reasonably straight poles for rafters. Before they are spiked into place, line them up together on a level surface near the ground so that you can walk around and even things out.  Take down any high points with a draw knife. As soon as you have them shaved decently straight, set the rafter poles, spike them in place, and space sheet across them for shingles.

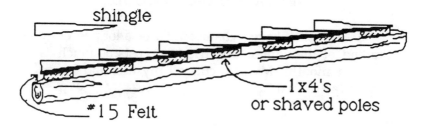

shingle

#15 Felt

1x4's
or shaved poles

With walls and roof in place, think about flooring. You could pour cement if you lived in downtown Burbank, but in Alaska, maybe you should think about wood. With finished, dimension lumber, set a level ridge around the bottom of the structure, and rest top-sawn logs (or cut lumber, if you can get it around these. Set two pieces of straight, finished lumber on the top, and run level lines across the top-sawn logs to make sure you don't have a high spot. Plywood flooring is best. Tongue and grooved 2X6's aren't bad. If you are way out in the boondocks, you will just have to chainsaw your own planking. They make an Alaskan Mill that will produce decent enough wood.

Either way you go, logs or log ends, you can finish both of these shells in a very quick time. Then crawl inside and sleep in a nice warm bed while the weather outside rages. Nothing aids the hunter-survivor like a cozy night's sheltered sleep, and these are absolutely two of the fastest ways to achieve it.

## THE HEAT'S ON---FIREWOOD

If I didn't have a chainsaw, I'd be a lot poorer by the end of the winter. Electric heat costs as much as $200 per month. My saw cuts all my fuel and I save about $1400 a year.

A chipper chain cuts firewoods with the best endurance. If you touch the ground under a log with your bar nose, or cut some dirty wood, it will dull a little, but still cut. Chisel chain will die on you.

Either way, you need to keep the chain out of the dirt. Since you are most often cutting on a long log laying on the ground, start on the right side of the log (right hand on the trigger) and, as you cut, move left so that the bar and chain are never in line with your body.

Again, think safety, or suture self. I really recommend chaps (four layers of ballistic nylon), which protect your legs from cuts and flying wood. Also, protect your ears and face, and don't forget your gloves.

Rev the saw up, and dig into the log. Cut down three fourths of the way, or until the saw begins to bind, whichever happens first. Then, let the CHAIN STOP WHILE THE BAR IS STILL IN THE WOOD. After you have made all the cuts on one log, roll the log over and finish the cuts by running back down the log. Again, move from right to left.

Firewood is about PRODUCING HEAT. Some body will stay warm because you cut, split and stacked wood. How you do all that determines how much heat you obtain.

Most writers don't express it this way, but it will help you to know that generally, heat production is measured by the pound; the heavier the wood, the more heat it contains. Also, heavy wood yields a slower, hotter burn, which keeps the heat in the stove instead of sending it up the chimney. Fir will produce only 64% of the heat contained in heavy Oak.

On the other hand, kindling should be made from a lightweight wood, most of which ignites easily and gives off quick heat. Therefore, cedar and other lightweight woods make good fire starters.

Don't burn green wood. Your wood must be dry to burn safely and efficiently. Safely means that it neither pops hot coals into your room, nor causes creosote deposits to gather in your flue, where they can later ignite and burn your house down. Efficiently means slow and hot.

Therefore, you need to cut and split the wood about six months before burning.

The smaller you split the wood, the quicker it will dry. By splitting the logs, you expose more surface to the air so moisture can escape.

You get about 80% of the heating capacity out of wood if it air drys for three months, and 90% of its heating capacity after a six month cure. Air drying means circulating dry air around the wood. If you merely throw it in a pile, it will dry slowly.

In almost all parts of the United States, you need protection from the elements. Keep your chainsaws sharp and during a cold winter, your bones will thank you. You not only will be indoors, out of the weather, but you'll have enough fuel to burn and keep the whole team comfortable.

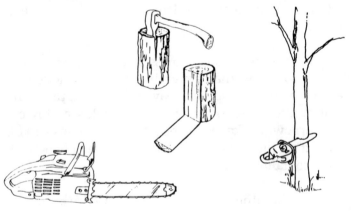

And now, the very best...

# Chapter 7

## ESCAPE & EVASION
## by
## SFC Brian Adams

*Editor's note on Brian Adams...*

*Like breeds of animals, some Special Forces people seem to be bred for a specific purpose. Brian's father was one of the legendary WW II Army Rangers who scaled the cliffs of Dover and fought the Germans. After the war, the family settled in the Missouri Ozarks, and Brian learned the woods. By the time he was eight years old, he could stay out hunting by himself for a few days and nobody would worry. He learned to whistle softly at deer so they would turn and expose a better shot, and he caught fish with his bare hands. He coped with every Ozark condition, and in his own words, "I've ate a lotta snakes."*

*After entering Special Forces, he was sent to SERE school, where he not only graduated, but was THE HONOR GRADUATE. He's the number one escape and evasion expert in the country, the very best.*

A note from Don...

**Would you be scared?** Suppose I chased you through the woods. You had no weapons, and I could carry any gun I wanted. Guess What? I'd get you. I spent a lot of time in Special Forces and I know how.

But then, let's stack the odds more in my favor. I get to use a few dogs, and a half-dozen well armed men. Now, you can be sure, your captured carcass would be mine.

But with dogs and well armed men, if I had to chase Brian Adams anywhere, I'd start the project by wetting my pants. This guy scares me; he knows every trick in the books, plus a few more he invented, and the guy is absolutely ruthless. I'd be scared stiff to chase him anywhere; he might catch me." --Don Paul

*****

This is what he told me:

In a few words, this is what it's about. They want to find you, and you fix it so they can't.

To find you, they have to use their senses. But you become one with your environment--- invisible and inaudible, so their senses won't work. Confuse them and they can't think, either. Attack them, harass them, trap them, destroy their minds, then their hearts, and finally some of their tired, beaten bodies, and the only thing that <u>will</u> work is their emotions. Then, you own them.

Stealth is your great ally. Speed is only used for emergencies. Many people think the idea in escaping and evading is merely to put distance between you and your pursuers. That's wrong--with one exception. In this game of life or death, stealth, and the ability to scheme are relative. It is them against you. In the beginning of the chase, flat out speed often works to your advantage, because it forces them into hot pursuit immediately, so they never get a chance to organize.

Even if you are running scared, so that the more lead time you have the better you like it, the answer may not be for you to run faster, but to make them run slower. Take at least one member of their party out, and the rest will slow down to a crawl. When they start out after you with superior numbers, better weapons and dogs, they will press on, and enjoy the chase. As soon as one of them dies, all will scare, and start thinking maybe this isn't fun after all.

DON'T PANIC; STAY COOL. If you fail in the panic department, you will lose your ability to scheme and plan. Once that happens and fear takes over, your major escape ability, that of scheming and planning, will disappear, and you're dead meat.

Chase is like chess. You have to know what power your enemy has on the board, and plan for every possibility. Don't just move. Think. Scheme. Consider, "What will happen if..?" Ambushes fail without knights on the flanks. Raids fail without rooks. The primary factor in escape & evasion (E&E) is your ability to PRECISELY assess the situation and then scheme and plan around the facts.

Never make a maneuver that requires a strength you don't have or a weapon you don't own. On the contrary, force them into over-extending, hurrying, and running scared. Why tangle with them when they are fresh, confident, and ready to fight. Wait. Sooner, or later, they will make a mistake.

The secondary factor is your physical condition and how well you maintain yourself as you escape.

Finally, distance is helpful, but remember
**ONLY HELPFUL...**

If you have a group of people chasing you, the ONLY reason for putting distance between you and them is to develop lead time. If you screw up and make distance your number one priority, you may forget to change directions, and any numbskull will be able to figure out where you are going, then cut you off and corner you. In Army SERE school, that's how the majority of prisoners were caught.

Another failure that results from too much distance is critical: You can't hurt them. Why should you let anybody chase you without paying? Injure a few, or kill one. When you're too far away from them, you can't do that effectively unless you happen to be a Phd trapper. So, remember, even though you may be running scared, distance may only be helpful.

To understand how to analyze your intel (intelligence equals everything you know about the enemy and the situation), use this list:

| THEY | YOU |
|---|---|
| How many? | How many? |
| How well armed? | How well armed? |
| Dogs?  Good? | |
| Other animals? | Animals? |
| Assets? | Assets |
| Radios, electronics | Rope? |
| Infa-red, Air? | |

Once this intel (information) is gathered, you can lead them a merry chase. Of course, you may also decide to destroy them.

Let's examine the possibilities: First, what good is lead time? Every trap you set, meal you eat, and weapon you build takes time, and the distance you put between you and them provides the time you need to work your magic. How much lead time would you like to have if you're scared? Lots. But cool it. To really know how much time you should develop has nothing to do with being scared. It depends on terrain, their ability and yours, and how long it takes you to set up a trap or an ambush. Of course, think about letting them overrun you, or circling around behind them. If dogs are part of the chase party, however, forget the thought.

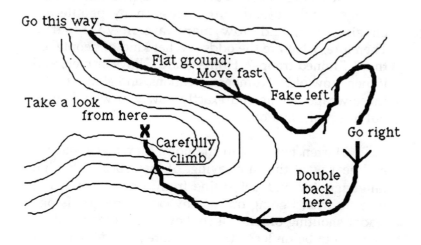

If they are right behind you, and the lead time is minutes, the situation provides you with an excellent opportunity to gather intelligence. Of course, you are on the run. As you make tracks, sooner or later you will come to a spur running off a hill. Double back on the other side of the spur, preferably along the military crest (easier climb, better cover).

When you think the time is right, cross over by crawling the last 100 meters on all fours to the peak of the spur. Even in darkness, it would be deathly foolish to silhouette yourself against a starlit sky.

Watch, and listen. Normally, they have superior numbers, so they won't be too careful about making noise. Just as they should, you must use your senses, but more important, use good sense. Note everything. Look for numbers, dogs, extra help, weapons, canteens, and clothing, but even the kinds of footgear they are wearing is important to you. Heavy boots mean they will have a difficult time running, especially in soft sand. Rubber soled tennis shoes mean they will be fast climbing rocky hills, but troubled on a hillside full of loose gravel.

If you've watched and listened, you know what you have to contend with. How many people are chasing you, and how many are in your party. Therefore, what are the odds? What kind of people are they? Trained troops? Home guard? Boys or men, and if men, how old? Numbers, weapons, and ability to use those weapons tells you exactly how you would come out in a confrontation.

Listen not only to the noise they make, but try and hear what they are saying. If they speak a foreign language, try and determine from tone of voice and volume what's going on. Is anybody arguing? Is one leader shouting orders? If so, how much pressure does he seem to be under? (In many foreign armies, failure to catch a prisoner results in severe punishment or even death.) If the leader chasing you is under pressure, he will press on too hard, and make mistakes, in which event, you can own his body.

If you can draw fire safely, do that. Don't even think about exposing yourself. But a lot of times you can set something up at night that will cause them to fire, especially after you have killed a few. They WILL be nervous, tired, and scared, which translates to trigger quick. Listen to the weapons. You can tell what they are shooting from the sound, which translates to range and firepower. With that information, you can plan winning engagements because you know how far and fast they can shoot effectively.

Of course, watch, but not too long. Cause the bad news is, when they are close, you may get caught, or, at the very least, shot at. NEVER risk getting cornered in a place from which you cannot easily escape.

110

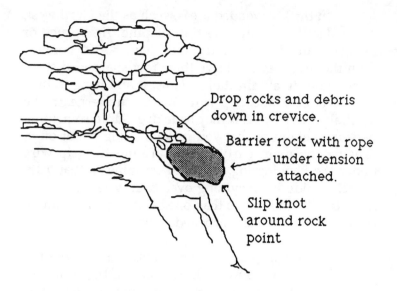

Drop rocks and debris down in crevice.

Barrier rock with rope under tension attached.

Slip knot around rock point

In rocky hills, get enough lead time to set up an avalanche tree. Double back to check them out. If they see you, they will start running up the hill, so boogie and cut the restraining rope as you leave.

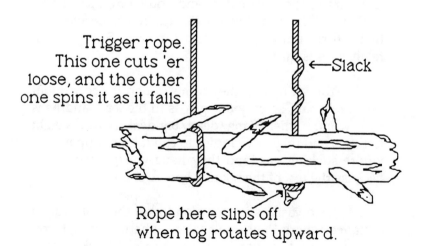

Trigger rope. This one cuts 'er loose, and the other one spins it as it falls.

←Slack

Rope here slips off when log rotates upward.

In thickly wooded areas, such as the Northwest, use a deadfall. Cut a section of pine, fir, spruce or hemlock out of a log. You should have 50-100 pounds. Trim the branches but leave three foot sharpened stubs sticking out in all directions. Hoist it and hang it, then set the trigger and trip-wire directly underneath the deadfall. Then leave. If they have dogs, drop something personal behind so that you make the dog poiint on it, causing the main party to mill around the trip wire under the hanging log. I like to set mine so that leafy branches hide it. Anything over twenty feet does just fine. It will land in less than one second, with maiming force as far out as the sharpened stubs.

I hate engaging an enemy, head-on. Every once in a while some hero decides that the three of you should kill the nine of them. They come up with this big plan: Ambush. It's risky, but they already made you mad, so your attitude thinks for you.

You figure the first three rounds out of your weapons will drop three, and you will have to fire fight with the other six. Odds then: two to one. If they suceed in taking cover, you withdraw, and they have to take care of their wounded, and you stung them badly so they will have to slow down, etc. You hope and pray that it turns out the way you planned it. Bull! How it really goes is this:

You set up and they come around the corner, but they are smart, so only one guy is in the lead, and he is their worst soldier. Bang/dead/big deal. Now it's eight to three, and they have radios to call for air support and you're sucking gas, and they have you pinned down because the rest of them know how to shoot. Disaster!

It's a vastly superior plan to kill them off from a distance where they don't know whether or not you stayed around to watch. I like no risk attacks; that's why I'm alive and they ain't.

112

How well they are armed has a lot to do with whether or not you fight. Of course, one shot out of any firearm will give away your position. Most often, though, you won't have a firearm with you, in which event you can consider using one of theirs. That plan is OK if the weapon you get from one of them will give you a range edge. (Range=distance the weapon shoots effectively. Edge=more than theirs.)

More often than not, however, you'll be stealing an AK-47, and since the rest of their team has the same weapon, you accomplish less than zip. You weigh add nine pounds in weight and deceive yourself by thinking you've gained an advantage. But really what you have done is match your one weapon against multiples of theirs--bad odds. Guns have the worst way of making us feel superior enough to fire---our one against their many. It's a much better plan to take one of their people out with a deadfall or trap, and keep on moving, but in a new, confounding direction.

The question, "good?" made the list because it's a comparative. How good are they compared to you? After reading this, you might know more, but who's in better shape? What if you are?

If you know that you can outrun them, do it. But not so fast. You need to change directions often so they can't figure out where you are going. Also, your advantage from being in better physical shape is not for putting distance between you, but for turning the physical aspects of the chase into a chess game in which you start out with an advantage.

Then what? Run them straight up a hill. When you get to the top, take a minute to plan a miserable descent. Look at the bottom and make sure that where you go they won't be able to see you. Plan on turning at the bottom to go unobserved through thick brush around a corner, then use flat out speed to get to another hill, where once again, you take them straight up, then straight down. If you develop some lead time, say, "Hello," with an avalanche greeting card, or set up a welcoming trip wire.

Listen to them as you do this. If you hear argument, gasping, coughing, or any sign of weakness, it may be time to let them overrun you so you can eliminate stragglers. Another opportunity may present itself in an all out race; generally one man will out distance all the rest. If he gets far enough in front of the main force, mangle him.

What if they have dogs? The good news is this: you might sometimes know where they are because some dogs bark. (The majority have been trained to be quiet on track, however.) If the tracking dogs bark, you will know what you have for lead time. Nothing gripes me more than starting a project I can't finish. You get halfway through making a trap, and you have to leave it. That tips your hand, and you can't be successful with the same trick twice.

Dogs are a big help to the enemy; you'll have to work around their ability. Contrary to how the movies go, you CANNOT fool a dog's nose; at best, you can disguise your scent and slow the dog down. Of course, no dog will overrun you. If you bury yourself in the woods or lie low in water, the dog will lead the whole pack of pursuers right to you.

But the handler is human, and he's essential to the dog because dog's don't work well with strangers. Don't try and defeat the dog; defeat the handler so you render the dog ineffective. At least divide and conquer; confuse the dog so that the handler loses confidence in the animal. If you can walk for any length of time on a railroad track, your scent will be harder to follow, especially after a moist, oxidizing night.

If several of you are trying to escape, their dog fastens in on only one scent. Keep circling out one member of your party at a time and learn whose scent the dog is following. Then, that member of the party splits off from the group in a hard to (visually) track spot, (rocks), and the rest of the group will go free.

Even at first if you can't eliminate the handler, you can make his life miserable. Take him through hell. He can't let the dog go because he can't keep up with it. That means the dog must be on a leash. Go into the worst brush you can find, and make several sharp turns. Guaranteed, the leash will tangle in the undergrowth, causing more frustration and delay than I can describe.

Dogs are either line (of smell) trackers or scent (trail) trackers. One works right behind you with his nose to the ground; the other works off a line-of-smell down wind from you with his nose in the air.

If the dog is a scent tracker, he stays right on your trail. Travel the most physically demanding terrain you can find. The dog will hold up fine; the handler won't. Dog handlers seldom stay in good physical shape--training the dog consumes long sedentary hours.

If the dog is a line tracker, he will trail downwind from your path. So, your turns should be mostly into the wind, especially when you want to lengthen lead time so you can trap them or, perhaps, feed yourself.

You can circle around and double back on a scent tracker. Just be careful not to circle too tightly, and keep a terrain feature between you and the posse as you do this. Don't, repeat, DO NOT try and circle back on a line tracker; he will pick up your scent and make an automatic change in your direction.

If they have attack dogs, think, "Kill." Once the dogs are away from the·handler on the attack, they pretty much belong to you. In First Blood, Rambo killed attacking dogs, but they never showed you how. He could have done it in a number of ways.

Pull this way to raise tip

Small stick, rope or string.

Charging dog impales here.

foot here

If they turn an attack dog on you, it will outdistance their main party. Once you kill the dog, take the heart and the hind quarters. It will be a great meal. Think of this, too. If the handler knows you will eat his dogs, he will hesitate to send another one after you.

Make a spear for the first. A barbed animal horn makes a great point, but the sharpened end of a stick will do just about as well. Sharpen not only both ends of your chosen wooden spear, but any side branches that happen to stick out, so that you can butt-stroke effectively into a dog's side.

In the event you lose your spear and one dog is still attacking, he may get to bite your left forearm, so wrap and tie it with bark, cloth, old boot tops, tin cans, or all of the above. The soft stuff goes next to your arm. Something the dog can sink his teeth into, like thick bark off a tree,  will be used for the outer wrapping. You need to make sure the dog holds his first bite. If he disengages, you lose, because he will bite again--- in a more tender, unprotected area.

Move your protected left (weak) arm as the dog approaches so that he goes for that moving part. Then swoop underneath into the belly with anything sharp. Make sure the weapon in your other hand stays hidden from the dog's sight, and move as fast as you ever thought you could when attacking. Too slow and the dog will release your forearm and bite your weapon hand with amazing speed. If you don't have anything to penetrate the dog's underside with, reach behind the head with your strong arm and pull in hard as your weak arm pushes out; the combined reverse pressure will snap the dog's neck.

Woodcroft (Silver Star Special Forces Medic) teaches hand-to-hand combat in Book I, and he makes it easy to learn because he sets it out by principle. At the risk of repeating, let me just define a weapon one more time with feeling. It is:
ANYTHING THAT LENGTHENS OR STRENGTHENS YOUR SPHERE OF DEFENSE

In order to do that, you must maintain:
POSITIVE CONTROL

In order for a weapon to be effective, it must be:
AN EXTENSION OF YOURSELF
so, your best spearing weapon is one which can be wielded from several different angles, and used to jab, swing, butt-stroke, club, block, and hook.

If you can stage the attack, you can set a trip wire that will impale the dog far away from you. Remember that dogs' keen sense of smell is the sense you need to fool. Any scent camouflage on a trip wire can help. Pulling it through wild animal or bird (owl) droppings, may get you past the dog's nose. If you have the time to do this, you can also set a trap that some man (without a dog's nose) will set off.

After scenting the trip wire, leave a personal item behind. The dog will go on point towards that item. Then, as man goes ahead to check out what the dog points at, he trips the wire. If it happens to be attached to a hundred pound dead fall twenty feet high, you may take out a couple of bodies, including the dog.

Incidentally, one of the great myths is that you can ruin a dog's nose with pepper. Not only does it NOT work, but it helps the dog since pepper makes it sneeze and clears out its nose so that all scents are new. You're far better off to leave the dog's nose alone. Like anything else, a dog's nose gets tired and wears down, so it's less effective as time rolls along.

Other animals might also have to be considered, not only for them, but for you. A horse, for example, makes travel easy, and gives the tracker a more distant view. If they have horses and dogs, take the horse up the side of a hill through the loosest shale or sand you can find, then go back down through the same kind of stuff. Horses hate that because horse sense tells the animal it could lose his footing.

Another excellent way to get away from a horse is to run through a forest of downed trees. You can crawl under. Horses can't.

Finally, in horse country, other animals will be around. Help yourself; but only if you have lead time. If you stay on horseback and run from them, it becomes an even chase. That's a bad deal. Any four-footed animal will transport you into high country. You can then dismount and send your animal one way, as you go another. Your path back down the hill goes under a maze of logs. That traps the posse's horses, so they are forced to trail on foot, detour, or ride back.

Incidentally, with good lead time and some aspirin, you can take them over ten thousand feet and they will suffer from HAPE (High Altitude Pulmonary Edema). If it doesn't bother you because you're in shape and they aren't, they will be relatively listless and easy to attack. They also may not know what is wrong with them OR how to treat it, which means the odds will shift drastically in your favor.

The last item you have to deal with is assets. Find out what they have. Any radios or electronic gear? Weapons, of course? In the beginning of any chase, watch out for a critical factor: air support. Air might be looking for you, which slightly changes your camouflage. If you even suspect that they have aircraft, or you think you hear one, NEVER go into open terrain. Stay covered and MOTIONLESS with any shiny parts, (like your hands and face) down and out of the light.

Likewise, never look directly at anybody who is looking for you unless you have a reason. Look away. If you don't believe that looking at somebody draws their attention to you, peek sideways at the driver next to you at a stoplight.

What about your assets? First, do you have basics, such as clothes and footgear. All the lead time you develop should be used to make sure you are equipped. Lots of tools, implements and weapons can be fashioned while you're on the move. You may need to make footgear, sunglasses, headgear, or clothes.

That's your first priority. ·If you allow yourself to be hurt, injured from the elements, or worn down, you have drastically reduced your ability to get away. More important, the tools and implements you come up with dictate your methods of attack and harrassment.

Think offense if you know they have air, and think about a uniform and weapon change. If you take theirs, you can fool air into thinking you are one of them and get an opportunity to destroy the aircraft and crew. Night attacks are fun, but you will have to neutralize their animal support first. Horses and dogs have a way of waking up easily.

*********

This is a good time to dispel a couple of myths:
**IF YOU GO UP IN THE TREES, THEY WILL MAKE A MONKEY OUT OF YOU. UNDERWATER HIDEOUTS ARE DISASTERS.**

As you sit at home and think about it, treetops are alluring. Here's the scenario: With a slingshot you shoot a shot-weighted fishline over a high limb. The fishline is tied to a parachute cord (500 lbs) and you pull it over. With your foot in the loop on one side of the line, you hand- over-hand up the other until you're into the tree tops. Then you connect tree to tree, and you befuddle the whole posse. Bull; it really goes:

You get up in the trees and, yes--the branches are thick enough to connect. It takes a while to pull this off so you lose lead time, and it is tiring. (Remember the work formula from Terrain Analysis.) Also, you could have fallen on your #&$% and broken something, but you made it! Now, you're ten-twenty trees away, and they arrive.

The dogs either bark tree'd or stop and look up. So the posse fans out and goes heads up also. You don't dare move. If you shoot, you'll kill one, and the other nineteen will ventilate you. You're cornered. They WILL find you, day or night, because they know you can't move. If you give away your position, (either move or shoot), they will kill you. Yes, the tree plan sucketh. I've tree'd and killed enough bear and racoon to be able to say with real authority---DON'T TAKE TO THE TREES.

Water is worse. Every war movie, from Rambo back, puts the hero into the drink. He breathes through a reed while they pass, and then comes out behind them. That's showbiz; here's real life:

You go into the water. If they have dogs, the doggie will turn and say, "This is where he went into the drink because I can't smell him anymore." (Even if you have bathed 100%, you develop maggot breath in the woods, and no dog could miss it.)

Then the handler will fan left or right and find a place for the dog to pick up your trail on one side of the bank or the other. If no trail, they know you continued to bathe. They will find you. "But," you say, "you're hidden under a bunch of sacred lilies, which they don't want to disturb, so they can't see you." (If you believe that, you will also believe Gary Hart is a celibate.)

So--they will just wait you out. Water takes away your body heat at a phenomenal rate, about 7 times as fast as air. Your natural body temperature is 98. Even if the water is a comfy 74, in time you will suffer from hypothermia. They'll wait, and wait, and you'll freeze.

Even if they don't have time to wait, (but they certainly will), detection is a big problem. You have to get deep enough so they can't see you through the water. You also have to breathe. Now, we already know that you wouldn't be in the water if you didn't believe in fiction, so you just happen to have with you a special camouflaged hose six feet long.

At first, you breathe fine. But then it becomes labored. Why? You exhale carbon dioxide, which does not clear the hose, so you breathe back in your own carbon dioxide, and re-use the unexpended oxygen. Like a submarine trapped on the bottom, you run out of air. You'll not only be cold, but sucking gas as you bubble to the top. Yes, water hideouts are great, but only in the movies...

Finally, there's the one about running in the creek. Then a scent dog can't track you and you get away. No, no.

First, you run a tremendous risk of injury travelling in creeks because all the rocks on the bottom are slippery. You'll think somebody designed them just for turning ankles. Second, you move more slowly in water than on land. Anybody can walk faster on the bank than you can wade in water. Hypothermia is also a problem, at the very least you lose calories, and therefore stamina. The creek getaway is an armchair dream; it won't work either.

****

Of course, you can't evade if you don't preserve yourself. If you let your diet go or get a mild case of food poisoning, you're history. You have to eat. No 7-11's are in the woods, so you will have to go native, and eat what's available.

If you have a chance to prepare a rucksack, and you know that you will be on the trail for a week or so, visit a health food store. I like Chia, pumpkin, and sunflower seeds, nuts, fruit and vegies (both dried), jerky, pemican, and powdered milk.

Most often in an E&E situation, however, you have to feed yourself on the run. Snakes, rodents and birds are great, but it takes a ton of lead time to catch them. You're better off with ants, termites and grubworms, because these are plentiful and take very little stopping time to catch and prepare. Even grasshoppers take some time to catch. Ants, termites and grub worms are the fast food of the jungle. Just think of this as the escapee's Kentucky Colonel. You can even sing, "We do termites right."

Turn over a rock and collect a bunch of ants on a leaf or piece of paper. Scoop them into a cup, add water, heat 'n serve. It will taste sweet. Break off a bottom chunk of wood to find termites, and flick these into the same cup. Incidentally, replace the log so the tracker won't know what you're eating. Add water, boil; enjoy.

Grub worms go down like a large pill. Break off the head, and swallow the body with a swig of water. These are best because the fat content provides you with energy.

With enough lead time developed to enable you to build a fire, you can upgrade your menu. Snakes, rodents, birds, wild pigs, squirrels, etc, make great meals. A fat rat isn't much less than a skinny rabbit. Poisonous snakes have to be pinned down with a forked stick and beheaded. How? Very carefully. I am not in favor of snakes because the risk isn't worth the low fat diet they provide, even though they are tasty. Birds can be snared alright, but they take a long time to prepare, and you have to boil any carrion-eater because they are full of parasites. Fowl are wonderful to eat, but they make a racket you would not believe when snared.

If you can obtain a chicken, you're in great shape, especially if you have a metal canteen or a metal ammo box for cooking. A hot fire will burn the pin feathers off. Now, cut or pull the body, gizzards and liver into pieces and stuff them into your canteen cup. Add wild rice or any vegie you can find. Fill with water. Boil in coals for about 30 minutes. Drink soup/eat pieces. Super- nutritious. I always thought they should make a TV commercial about it being a great way to start the day.

# DRY RIVER BED

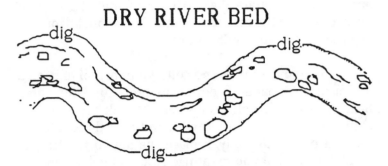

DRY RIVER BED
GREAT PLACE TO DIG FOR WATER.
Dig on the outer edge of the river bed. Put
a still in the sun.

You can run for a long time on almost no food, but you must have water. DO NOT allow yourself to become dehydrated. As you hit the bottoms of various mountains, replenish your supply of water before climbing back up. Even in a dry stream bed, water can generally be found a few feet below the surface on the outside circumference of the stream's bends. If you have enough lead time, find such an outside bend on which the sun shines, and build a solar still.

As long as we are thinking about water, let's remember fish. On a field problem in Colorado, I fed our whole team 89 fish in four days, all of which I caught by hand.

Walk slowly up to a clear stream and observe where the trout swim into a hole after they see you. Under a rock or a log, the fish may have another way out. Find the escape hole and block it; then follow this procedure: Wade in, block the hole with your chest, and reach in after them. Allow the temperature of both hands to drop down to water temperature (generally numb), and reach slowly into the hole on both sides of the fish. Work your hands gently from the tail to the head. Squeeze firmly, and toss him on the bank.

A stick jammed into the fish's body through the mouth can be propped level over the fire and turned. Although raw ocean fish is OK, fresh water fish often carry parasites, so cook thoroughly.

After dinner, throw the remains back into the water. Why let them know how you're dining? They want to hurt you; the less they know the better. Besides, tidy housekeepers slow trackers down; with no sign, it takes them longer to try and figure things out.

Crawdads are about the tastiest outdoor meal around, and they are fairly easy to catch by hand. You can also make a crawdad trap or spear them.

Don't forget to eat your greens. You need a balanced diet now more than ever. Grass is OK, but don't eat the kind with the rough edges (it screws up digestive system), and some of the lawn varieties are cut. DO NOT eat any plant with a milky sap, except for dandelions, which are fine. You're much better off to spend the time and effort to learn exactly what's good for you and what isn't.

Above all, work at good health habits, and eat to keep your energy high.

(WRITER'S NOTE) Here are Brian's answers to some specific questions:

PATHFINDER: What's the best number of escapees? ANSWER: Three. Two sleep; one watches. One diverts, two ambush. One leads, two circle around. One injured, two carry. CHOOSE GOOD PEOPLE! We spent tedious chapters in Book I of this series telling you how to choose good team members. Don't take anyone who doesn't measure up.

PATHFINDER: What's the best time to travel?

ANSWER: Travel by night; lay up by day, generally. If they have lights and dogs, they can move faster through terrain, but without dogs, it's harder to track at night. Don't bust your #&%$@ trying to move too fast at night. Also, don't get into a time schedule rut that let's 'em know when you move and when you sleep.

PATHFINDER: What about sleep?

ANSWER: Sleep is very important. I think up the best schemes when I am fresh. Sleep ALWAYS where the terrain approach forces them to make warning noises. Sleep so that you have a good view of your back trail. As dusk turns to darkness watch and listen before you move into your sleeping area. When you're sure no one is around, slip in just after dark and set up your bedding. Knowing that you are hidden, and that the approaches are noisy, you'll sleep like a baby.

PATHFINDER: Should you split your party in half?

ANSWER: Dumb; 12 TO 2 odds are much better than six of them against one of you. You double your mistake potential, and weaken your fighting force. Never split a buddy team.

PATHFINDER: What if the encircle you?

ANSWER: You travelled too far in a straight line. If they tighten the circle, you are in deep whale puckey. But that's spilt milk. Probe the circle to get out. If you don't succeed, withdraw and try another probe elsewhere. If you get close to their outer perimeter at night, and they don't have dogs, bury yourself and let them overrun you.

PATHFINDER: What if there is only one tracker?

ANSWER: Travel line abreast. It slows down the tracker, and the main force doesn't dare go ahead of him.

PATHFINDER: I hunted in Oregon with Charlie Phillips, the chief biologist for the Siuslaw National Forest Service. He used to make himself smell like the plants the elk lived in, and he got right up on them. Wouldn't scent camouflage work with dogs?

ANSWER: You're talkin' the difference between preyed-upon and predator. Dogs are predators, and they don't fool that easily.

126

# Chapter 8

Becoming invisible outdoors...

# CAMOUFLAGE

Each year, statistics show an increase in crime. Even in prosperous times, your chances of becoming a victim are scary.

But when times get tough...watch out! We've trained several generations of people to expect something for nothing (welfare). Their attitudes are not going to change just because we ran out of support money. Thus, it's a safe bet to assume, a lot more people out there will want to rob and plunder you.

But if they can't find you, they can't hurt you. Therefore, the art of camouflage is a great survival skill. It's also great to know if you like fine, inexpensive dining. In Oregon, I brought home an extra 600 lbs. of bear and deer (fine, lean meat) every year. That's a $1,200 annual savings (tax free). But you have to camouflage yourself three ways in order to score.

Most of us believe that humans are gifted with five senses. I don't believe that; I think we have six. The five common senses are: Sight, hearing, smell, taste and touch. Obviously, camouflage doesn't deal with the last two, so camouflage is the art of concealment from sight, sound detection, and smell.

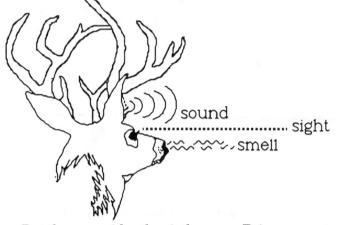

But then, consider the sixth sense. Drive up next to someone at a stoplight, and stare at them. They will discover you. Their sixth sense sends a message: "Intruder." So, whether you are being stalked or stalking, DON'T STARE AT YOUR ENEMY. Avoid their sixth sense.

## SCHEMING AGAINST SIGHT

In camouflage, the "DO NOT's" are often more important that the "DO's."

### DON'TS

DON'T move. The eye---especially the eye of a predator, be it dog or man or horse, picks up on movement. To stay undiscovered, don't move. I had a hateful neighbor in Oregon once who spent a lot of time spying on me. I would jerk my head in his general direction, and the chicken liver would duck everytime.

DON'T color clash. This book is not camouflaged. It's designed to clash 'n flash on a buyer in a bookstore full of other nice red and blue covers. Rub a little dirt on the cover to remove the shine and toss it in the grass, however, and it's harder to see.

(Don't worry about damaging a book. These books are guaranteed for life. Pathfinder will send a new copy to a former owner for an old cover and $4.50)

DON'T EVER---SILHOUETTE yourself against a skyline, or a clear lake on a moonlit night, or a doorway, or a window, or any kind of light. You may have played it cool, dressed in black, smeared your face, and stayed in the shadows, but if you appear before a bright background of any kind, look down to see if a little red dot is bouncing around on your clothing.

## DO:

Break up your outline. If I am looking for a helmet, and you are wearing a bush around your head, I won't notice you. Are you trying to hide in a warehouse..? Tape cardboard around your arms and legs. Maybe wear a box over your head with two small holes for your eyes.

Make your coloring match your surroundings. Blend in; don't stand out. We have concrete colored uniforms now for anti-terrorists. If you wouldn't think of wearing blue jeans to a black tie wedding, why would you wear green BDU's (battle dress uniforms) against desert sand?

Blend into your background. In your white bunny suit, stay against snow, not a black tree. Once you have chosen a way to dress, don't venture into an area that doesn't match your outfit.

Camouflage all the clothes you wear. Everything. You never know when you might be operating in your skivies. Way back when I was in high school, I was chased in East Los Angeles by some jealous, knife wielding people I had offended. I had worn a white shirt and brown pants that night. I ditched the shirt, because it was summer and I was tanned. In the shadows, they couldn't see me, and I never smiled.

Successful camouflage employs a chain of deception. Just like a chain, the weakest link gives it away. If you dress up in all the right clothing, and you don't do anything to your hair, face, hands or shoes, you'll be easy to see. Humans sweat, and in that sweat is oil. So, the first thing that happens to the backs of your hands and your face is that it gets an oil covering--- thus making it reflect light. Don't let it shine; paint your face, or rub a little dirt on it. Same with any beard you might have. Wash the backs of your hands with dirt, and hide all shiners, such as a wrist watch.

Of course, if you camouflage your body really well, but then drive a shiny red jeep, you haven't done much. Almost everywhere you go, you will take your vehicle with you; camouflage it. Do the same with your storage, boat, and your home. The fewer people who see you, or anything you ride or live in, the better off you are.

In the early days of warfare and hunting, we used to take the shine off our skin by using a variety of field expedients. We scrubbed our faces and hair with dirt, and used mud on the backs of our hands. If time allowed, we tied small bushes into a headband, and hung some greenery on our clothes.

Today, you can buy everything you need. Several mail order houses notably Brigade Quartermaster in Marietta, Georgia, and US Cavalry, 1375 N Wilson Rd, Radcliff, Kentucky 40160, carry some of the best, and you can get a free color catalog so you can see what the stuff looks like.

Try the new stretchy cheescloth for over the head, (covers face AND hair) and you don't have to worry about sweating body oil through camouflage paint on your face. They sell a watch band with a flap that locks over the face of your watch, and camouflage tape to cover the stock of your rifle.

Remember, the weakest link will give you away. Study yourself in a full length mirror, with all your gear, before leaving. If everything is done right, but you forget one shiny piece of jewelry or a worn shiny sight ramp on your rifle, you might as well wear a business suit with a flashy tie.

## SCHEMING AGAINST SOUND

We call the camouflage of sound, "noise discipline." To do this really right, you need ears with the capability of your enemy's. If someone is seriously looking for you with serious intent to do damage, they will probably use an audio-booster of some kind. Test your own team by using a similar device.

That's also a good idea if you want to hunt. Almost all animals hear better than man. Without electronically boosted ears, learn not to make noise out of context. Wear soft clothes so that brushing against a tree limb doesn't send a wrong message to your wilderness neighbors.

131

Do the same with smell. Begin by bathing as well as you can, and then wear CLEAN clothes, fresh off the line. Dental hygiene is also important. You can buy all kinds of commercial buck lures; I used to use one from Herters mixed with apple scent. To me it smelled good. Whether you are hunting or being hunted, the rule is NO TOBACCO. Humans can smell it up to two miles away downwind, and it freaks wild animals out.

If an enemy is looking for you, and they have airplanes, carry a survival net. You can hear them long before they can see you, and all you have to do is drop to the ground and throw the net over yourself. A camouflaged hammock will do just about as well, especially if the body hiding under it is properly outfitted.

Learn to fool sight, go through the woods quietly, and keep oral and body odors to a minimum. In good times, you'll have meat on the table, and in bad times, they will think you left the country.

*EVERY Green Beret is an expert at carrying all his gear on his back. Getting his "stuff" together is his first and foremost operational skill, so much so, that you often hear, "rucksack time" used to mean "Go to war!"*

*Still, everybody has special tricks and special preferences. If you made a list compiling everybody's special take-alongs, you would need a Mac Truck. The hardest part of this writing job was eliminating articles in order to cut the list down to something manageable. Guaranteed, you will have the same problem when you pack your rucksack. It becomes a question of ounces if you carry it, and a question of weight and volume versus utility if you travel by carrier.*

*Here then, is a starter list of survival equipment. Add and subtract according to your own preferences.*

# Chapter 9

Getting ready to hit the hills...
### WHAT TO TAKE WITH YOU
by
A team of Green Berets who agreed,
...almost.

**LIBRARY**
Bible
First Aid Manual and/or Medical Home
Encyclopedia
Green Berets' Guide to Outdoor Survival, Vols I,
II.Back issues of Mother Earth News.
Boy Scout Handbook
Other assorted, specialty survival books.

## OFFICE SUPPLY
Pens and pencils, paper, pocket-size note pads.
Magnifying glass or spectacles.
Hand-held calculator. Spare batteries.
Luxury--small computer.

## FIRE STARTING AND FUEL EQUIPMENT
Wood matches and paper matches (mostly wood).
Cigarette lighters. (Lightweight bics are fine.)
Lanterns, (Oil, white gas or kerosene).
Candles (big, and birthday variety).
Metal (magnesium, flint) fire starter
and roadflares.
Fire extinguisher(s). (High pressure water refill.)

## CUTTING GEAR
Folding belt knife, and/or hunting knives.
Axes. Extra handle(s).
Sledge hammer. Extra handle(s).
Machete, and/or bolo knife.
Scissors.
One hand saw, (8 point); one bow saw.
Chainsaw 16-20" bar. Gas-mix oil, bar lube, files,
sharpening gear. Chain, safety gear, etc.
Wood splitting.. mauls, wedges, 5 pound ax.

## MEDICAL AID
Standard First Aid kit. (Anti-biotics).
Two year supply prescription &
counter medications.
Air splints.
Thermometer and Blood pressure tester.
Several small, first aid kits.
Snakebite kits.

## BARTER SUPPLY
Gold, Silver, popular ammo, labor skills.
Pre-1964 silver coinage, U.S.
Tools usable in your geographic survival area.

## HEALTH & HYGIENE.
Dental care (floss, toothpaste, brushes, etc.)
Soaps, shampoos, towels, washclothes.
Water purification systems--tabs, straws, filters.

## TACTICAL GEAR
Binoculars. (one 7 X 50mm).
Spotting Scope. Tripod.
Shotgun microphone.
Camouflage, make-up & scent. (Buck lure)
Compasses.
Stopwatch/calculator.
Flashlights for signaling, with colored lenses.
Tape--adhesive, camouflage, and electrical.

## WEAPONRY
Shotgun, rifle, and pistol chosen from
Chapter 2.
Small bore rifle, pistol. Case of ammo. (variety)
Reloading gear, ammunition, dies,
bullets, powder.
Extra parts, magazines, and cleaning gear.
Special sighting systems.
Thin strip adhesive tape with flourescent pens.
Kevlar clothing (bullet proof).
Luxury--crossbow with arrows, etc.
 silenced .22 auto pistol.

## OUTDOOR GEAR
Tents. Cots. Tent repair. (patches)
Mosquito netting, sleep and headnet.
Load-bearing gear, web belt and canteens
for climate.
Day or UZI pack, with gear.
Rain gear, (poncho), and poncho liner.
Boots for your terrain. (Booties for ocean coral).
Gloves--work, leather, and anti-cold.
Headgear. (hats, helmets, caps.) Sunglasses.

Thermal underwear.and socks.
Space blankets.
Sleeping bag. (with Holofil, not Down.)
Eating utensils, cooking gear, collapsible cups.
Sewing kit, awl and heavy leather
stitching thread.
BACKPACK, LARGE. Choose interior/
exterior frame.
First Aid pack.
Lightweight ammo.
Wire saw.
Swiss Officers' Knife, with small
sharpening stone.
Fire starter.
Camouflage clothing, headgear.
Socks and underwear.
Eating utensils, collapsible plastic cups, mess kit.
Entrenching tool.
Binoculars.
Flashlights and batteries (one small).
Parachute cord.
Extra compass. Topo maps.
Fish line for snares.
Small health and hygiene pack.
Running, tennis, or mountain climbing
(canvass) shoes.

## CONSTRUCTION &
## HOMESTEADING GEAR.
Hammers, nails, belt and bag(s),
tape (measuring), lines and squares.
Gas generator, 110 watts.
Electric grinder, with steel brush wheel.
Plumbing tools/glue. Plastic pipe & fittings.
Electricians' tools and 300 feet 14/3 wire.
Luxury--Air compressor for nail guns, air
wrenches, paint.
Electric saw (generated) with 6 blades & flat file.

## MISC TOOLS AND HARDWARE
Nut, screw, and bolt set.
Glue and adhesives--15 packages, variety.
Wrenches, screwdrivers, sockets, ratchets, etc.
Ropes in various lengths, materials, pulleys.
Luxury--Baker tree stand, climbing gear.
(extra bulbs)

## COMMUNICATION GEAR
Signal mirror.
Walkie Talkies. (5 watt)
Scanner monitor.
Short Wave receiver. AM and FM Bands, too.

## FOOD
Jerky, pemmican, dried vegetables, fruit.
Seeds, nuts, grains, rice.
Canned goods, made at home.
Package freeze dried foods or C rations.
Powdered or soy milk.
Soybean by-products.
Vitamins, and more vitamins.
Luxury--freezer.

## HUNTING AND FISHING GEAR
Spear, mask & snorkel, fins, game bag, gill net.
Rods and reels for local fishing, tackle
box 'n gear.
Traps, snares, and animal lures (salt licks.)
Compound bow, arrows, quiver, finger-tab,
arm guard.
Rifle, with scope and ammo.

## LAND TRANSPORTATION
Four-wheel drive vehicle, with utility trailer.
Road maps and atlas.
Trail (low gear) motorcycle.
Mountain Bicycle.
Ani-mules?

## WATER TRANSPORTATION
Canoe and paddles.
Aluminum cartop boat, or, Rubber inflatable.
Luxury--outboard engine, tanks, hoses, etc.
Water charts.

## LIBRARY
Bible heads the list. It replaces 250 psychology,
self help and other fad books. The older I get,
and the more I read great books, the more I
appreciate this, the Book of books. The Red
Cross puts out a great first aid manual and it's
cheap. Mother Earth News is good, practical
reading. The best all-around outdoor manual is
published by the Boy Scouts. A host of Army
books are cheap and fairly easy to obtain.

## OFFICE SUPPLY
Stuff to write with, keep notes on and pencils
and pens. A hand-held calculator is a must for
figuring demolition charges, lumber lists, basic
trigonometry, etc. If you want to live in luxury,
get a computer and learn how to use it.

## FIRE STARTING EQUIPMENT
Be able to make a fire anywhere, and be able to
put it out. Lanterns light up the night, and
birthday candles kill mosquitos in your tent.

## CUTTING GEAR
Slicing, dicing, and cutting wood to size will
always be necessary. The folding knife stays
with you always, and I have used mine in places
where I never thought to carry one. Put good set
in your eight point saw, and keep your bow saw
oiled. As you will read elsewhere, if you have a
chainsaw you can make almostanything.
Nothing beats a good hunting knife. I use mine
in the kitchen every day, so I am familiar with it.
It's the first thing I pack for the trail.

## MEDICAL AID

Woodcroft (Special Forces medic author in Book I) points out that Americans are the only people in the world who have lived in health so long and had doctors available so frequently that they don't prepare. You can learn the basics in a week. Take a course, and spend the money for equipment. It's really high priority. Then, if you want to do dangerous things in the woods, suture self.

## BARTER SUPPLY

This is a toughie. Get what will be valuable after an economic crash, etc. Gold will always work, but rather than the metal, I like a dredge or at least a gold pan.

## HEALTH AND HYGIENE

You're not a survivor if you get sick and die. It all starts with taking care of yourself. Like your mom told you, "Brush your teeth, take a bath, and don't drink dirty water."

## TACTICAL GEAR

Survival often means conflict with other humans who want what you have. In conflict, you will either have to win or negotiate, and you can't do either effectively if you don't know what's going on. Enhance your sensory capacity with optics. The 7X50 mm binoculars are better for night use. Spotting scopes on tripods have greater optical power; mine zooms to 36X. Use an audio booster. Listening to conversations and animal sounds from a long distance provides you with a lot of knowledge about your environment. Flashlights with interchangeable lenses enable you to share intelligence (via morse code signal) with fellow team members, or charge your fluorescent gear for easy night identification.

Of course, while you want to know about your surroundings, you want your surroundings to know nothing of you. Wear musk taken from a deer's organs.

## WEAPONRY

You need spare parts and ammunition. So, you either buy ammo by the ton, or keep the components (primers, powder) stored. The latter method is safer and easier. Learn to reload. Buy dies and bullet molds, and acquire a melting pot with casts. Don't forget gas checks.

Not only is reloading safer and cheaper, but it allows you to constantly upgrade your ammunition. Using a semi-wadcutter in a .357, I once shot a bear in the face with rather poor results, so I quit using that bullet and started loading with hollow points. If you're getting too much brush deflection with spitzers, change to round nose bullets. Of course, shotgun patterning and efficiency can be altered with different wads, pressure or shot sizes.

If you have a night rifle scope for your weapons, go with that. You'll burn quite a bit of midnight gun powder. Without special sights, learn the PAUL stance (Book I) and use adhesive tape with fluorescent marker on the top of your gun barrels for left/right direction.

In the luxury department we find crossbows and silenced small bore pistols. Be careful in practice. Silencers are illegal and crossbows can't be used on game. Confiscation is the common law enforcement practice.

## OUTDOOR GEAR

Make a tent at home from a kit. That's best.
Otherwise, consider whether or not you will

carry it in a vehicle or in your ruck, and buy
accordingly. You can live in the woods without a
tent, though, and do just fine.

What you can't get caught without is netting. In
many places, mosquitos will eat you alive, and
in some jungles, they transmit malaria. You
must have bed netting and a head net for hiking.

I don't carry my big ruck with me everywhere I
go. I scout, fish, hunt, and forage with only a
day pack. The major ruck gets cached. For
combat, a UZI pack is probably better, but either
way, you need something besides your major
backpack load for daily excursions.

Space blankets (I carry three) are a high priority
item. Increase your sleeping bag's efficiency by
using the blankets to sandwich your bag.
Incidentally, down bags need dry cleaning, and
the Naptha often used in that process can kill
you, if you zip up into the bag on a cold night.
How convenient; your sleeping bag becomes a
body bag. I buy only holofill bags, and I wash
them in soap and water myself.

Footgear is important. I like three changes on a
long hike, and I will carry them; I don't care
what they weigh. Noted outdoor writer
Bradford Angier once wrote that extra weight on
your feet was a lot more taxing than extra pack
weight. That's true. So, if you need to boogie,
you won't want six pounds on your feet, and
you want the rubber soles to reach down and

141

grab your path, whether it's rock or sand. (See Backpack, below). Changing footgear to fly across sand or scoot up a rocky hillside is like being able to change tires on a jeep to match the terrain; it really gives you an advantage. Also, you need special shoes to protect your feet if you go into water.

## BACKPACK, LARGE.

We are talking about your backpack, your personal ruck. Mine is ready almost always, stuffed with tightly rolled clothes and a variety of gear I use everywhere. Since I fly a lot, I don't carry ammo or weapons, but I do carry three fire starters, even in the tropics. Carry clean eating utensils, (plastic forks, etc., from fast food places).

The Army makes a folding shovel (entrenching tool) and a good plastic carrying case. File one side rather sharp, and you can use it as a two-handed machete. Parachute cord breaks down into strong, usable string. Topographic maps for your area provide ultimate intelligence. Monofilament fishing line has lots of uses, from snares to trip wires.

Wrap a meter or so of duct tape around your rucksack frame. You can use it to repair and fabricate all kinds of stuff. Six safety pins, alligator clips, and shower curtain rings provide huge convenience for almost zero weight. Hang them from your zipper fobs, perhaps. A few double duty trash bags also weigh little, keep all gear dry in a storm. One pack of unwaxed dental floss with sewing needles will stich up anything, including your leg in an emergency.

Finally, wait until your toilet paper at home is down to almost zip. Remove the roll, flatten it and throw it in your pack. It blows noses, stops bleeding, STARTS FIRES beautifully, and provides convenience.

## CONSTRUCTION AND HOMESTEADING GEAR.

Everything you need to put shelter together. If you don't know how to use it all, add a couple of books to your library for reference.

## MISC. TOOLS AND HARDWARE

One good way to gather the nuts 'n bolts is to buy the kits, about $30-40 each from DRI. I bought several and found them all useful. Otherwise, go to flea markets and swap meets and get it all together. The key to organizing is in owning the containers with slide drawers and labels. Also, get a Rolodex and use color cards matched to painted areas of your garage or workshop. Alphabetically list the tool or part, and the color sends you to the correct area.

## COMMUNICATION GEAR

Signal mirrors and Walkie Talkies are great ways to stay in touch with home base. A scanner pulls up all the important Fire and Police calls so you know what's happening as soon as it happens. Short wave receivers with AM and FM bands should be portable. Spare batteries allow you to live in the woods and know what's happening.

## FOOD.

Our ideas are different. We don't intend to become cooks out there, because we are not cooks here. Eating is not the focal point of our lives. Health food stores sell a book by Paavo Airolo (sp?) who thinks it's best to contain your

diet to seeds, nuts, grains, fruit and vegetables.
All of the above can be eaten without cooking,
and it is completely nutritious. Since we like
meat, we eat bear, venison, fish foul and reptiles.
Cook wild game meat thoroughly and avoid
parasites!

## HUNTING AND FISHING GEAR
Most survival schools try and solve the problem
with tons of ammunition and guns. No, no.
They may not only be unnecessary, but make
noise and disclose your position.

If you read <u>HABITAT</u>, you know that lots of
survival retreats exist all over the world where
food can be obtained by hand. In the Islands, for
example, you can be twice as productive with
underwater hunting gear. We find that the best
combination is a heavy-duty spear gun for
distance shooting or big fish, and a pole spear
with a three prong nose that spreads out when
you hit the fish. Make sure to hang your game
bag on a float bottle off a 30' line attached to
your dive belt. That way, un-invited dinner
guests merely tug on you waist as opposed to
taking a chunk out of your body. If you don't
swim, or sharks bother you, use rods 'n reels,
hooks 'n bait.

A compound bow is a silent tool for bringing
home dinner. Five other guys and I drove along
a mountain road in a truck with a sharp-eyed kid
who would spot deer laid up under a tree in the
heat. When he saw one, we would drop off a
few bowmen on each side to converge on the
tree. A four point buck charged out right at me,
and I let an arrow fly, but he jammed left just as I
shot. I thought the arrow went through his most
delicate parts, but in reality, I cut both afteries in

the rear hams, and the blood trail was easy to follow. I shot that buck in season and tagged it properly, (I hope). But hundreds of obsure laws "control" sportsman, so even better, a bow means no game warden will hear the shot. Compound bows are great for providing food without announcing to the whole world what's going on.

Finally, traps can be purchased cheaply at flea markets. Boil in water and let rust to kill all scent. Then don't handle them unless you wear gloves. If you decide to trap in a big way, buy a separate book on it, and learn to use space blankets that you fold together with your body scent inside. Practice with snares and lures. If you climb with a tree stand and take your bow and arrow, a 5 pound salt lick should draw dinner into arrow range.

## TRANSPORTATION
Think budget here because a four-wheel vehicle is expensive. A utility trailer, on the other hand, is cheap, so if you are poor, do as I did. I bought a truck with a trailer hitch and a posi- traction rear end; then I went to a junk yard and paid $25 for used air shocks.

On a four-wheel drive vehicle, only two wheels pull. Posi-traction also gave me two wheels pulling, and I never noticed the difference. I loaded my utility trailer so the tongue was heavy, and the traction was great. The rig was entirely adequate, and it cost a third of what a comparable four-wheel drive was selling for.

Bikes go places your truck can't, and they use no gas, so throw one in the trailer. I love a mountain bicycle. It makes zero noise on a mountain paved road. With ten speeds and balloon tires, you can pedal anywhere. Horses, mules and dogs all carry a load, and they are more compatible with your environment than anything gas powered.

This is a checklist chapter. If your retreat habitat is well defined, modify the list to take care of what you will need for your environment. Water bags would be a great addition for the desert, but forget snow shovels.

Once you've assembled the gear on this basic list though, you have a much better chance of surviving--anywhere.

# INDEX

# EVERYBODY'S KNIFE BIBLE

Two typical illustrations. This book ties in with our latest *Never Get Lost* We show you how to use a knife to tell what time it is, measure a cliff for the right amount of climbing rope, or figure a safe river crossing. But there's more. This book is considered by many to be the premier knife-use book in the world. Over thirty thousand knife-users from all over use this book. Shouldn't you? **$12.95**

## HOME MADE HOLDING BLOCK FOR BIG STONE OR DIAMOND

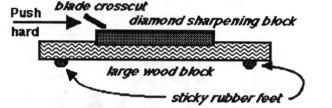

Push hard → *blade crosscut*

*diamond sharpening block*

*large wood block*

*sticky rubber feet*

You can bring your blade's edge to perfection, but first, you have to hold the whetstone steady. Make a big wood block to create a perfect knife edge.

## FORWARD LIGHT FROM YOUR KNIFE SHEATH LIGHTS YOUR PATH

**Light forward angle at 15°**

"Your Word is a lamp to my feet and a light for my path."

*Psalms 119:105*

How would you like to be ushered through the woods at night? If you modify your sheath loop the way we show you, your knife will hang forward at a15° angle. Taping a pen light on the top of your sheath will then allow you to flip a switch and light up the woods or jungle floor in the dark. We show you how.

## CUTTING ANGLES FOR VARIOUS USES

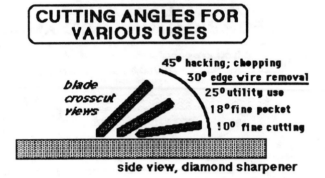

blade crosscut views

45° hacking; chopping
30° edge wire removal
25° utility use
18° fine pocket
10° fine cutting

side view, diamond sharpener

## CERAMIC SHARPENING STICKS

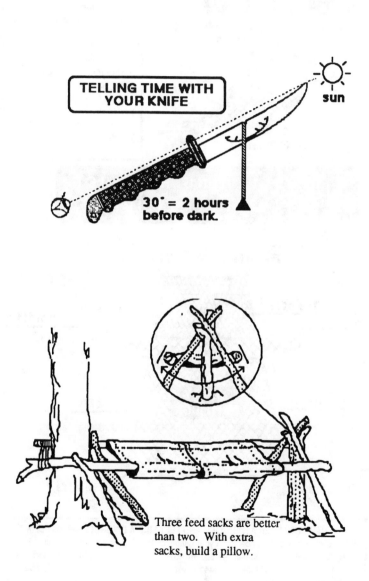

**TELLING TIME WITH YOUR KNIFE**

sun

30° = 2 hours before dark.

Three feed sacks are better than two. With extra sacks, build a pillow.

## A FEW USEFUL HAMMOCK THINGS
### to make roughing it super-easy

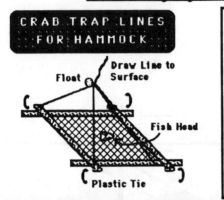

**CRAB TRAP LINES FOR HAMMOCK**

Float
Draw Line to Surface
Fish Head
Plastic Tie

**YOU'LL APPRECIATE** fresh crab in the woods. It's easy to prepare and will satisfy any stomach with run-away hunger problems.

Catch all you need in muddy water with your **hammock.** In these pages, we show you other ways you can use your hammock. You'll feed yourself like a king while camping near any lake or river you find in the boonies.

**HIGH SLEEPING HAMMOCK SAFETY PROCEDURES**

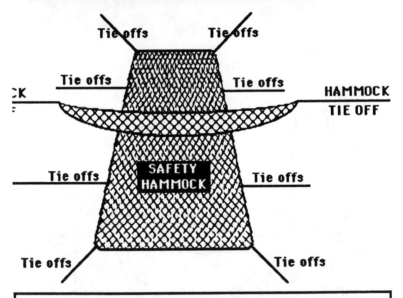

Tie offs          Tie offs

Tie offs          Tie offs

⊃K                                    HAMMOCK
⊃                                      TIE OFF

Tie offs          Tie offs

**SAFETY HAMMOCK**

Tie offs          Tie offs

**HAVE YOU USED A HAMMOCK AND FELT LIKE A DIVORCEE-----DUMPED?**
In this book, we show you how to tie your hammock together so you can't fall out. For extra safety high up in a tree, however, we add---another hammock or two. The first stretches under you so you can't fall. The second hangs over you like a camouflage net, so nobody but a monkey knows you're there.

## TEAR OUT OR COPY THIS PAGE
## USE YOUR PRODUCT REBATE COUPONS JUST
## LIKE CASH WHEN YOU ORDER FROM PATH FINDER

Path Finder's product rebate coupons (reverse side) can be used as cash at most of our dealers or by mail order from Path Finder Publications on any of the following:

**24 + WAYS TO USE YOUR HAMMOCK IN THE FIELD.    $4.95**
We actually figured out over two dozen ways to use this versatile, light weight tools in the woods. It will camouflage you, feed you like a king, and hold your rifle and binoculars steady. We filled one with rocks and knocked a trapped truck off a hill. Easy to read, we show you how to do it all with photos and illustrations.

**NEVER GET LOST. P.A.U.L. system. $9.95** The Green Beret's Compass Course. Reviewed by almost every major outdoor magazine, this book contains your land navigation system of the future. You can go anywhere, anytime, **without a map**, and never get lost. We've sold over 25,000 of these and have hundreds of testimonial letters.

**EVERYBODY'S KNIFE BIBLE.    $12.95** First reviewed by the *AMERICAN SURVIVAL GUIDE MAGAZINE.* They called it "innovative, funny, and sixteen of the most inventive and informative chapters on knives and knife uses ever written." Over 30,000 copies sold. This is **the book** you need to perform like a woods-king in the outdoors. Don't buy another knife until you've read this! .

**EVERYBODY'S OUTDOOR SURVIVAL GUIDE. $12.95** The Green Beret's Guide to Outdoor Survival. Over 15,000 in print with great reviews. This book teaches you survival arts as if you were on a Green Beret team. Best shooting instruction around for all weapons. It has Woodcroft's hand-to-hand combat methods, water purification. Also, how to double your survive-ability with help from animals, plus more.

**THE COMPLETE SELF DEFENSE MANUAL** by Huber. **$12.95** Covers ways and means to protect yourself and family. Takes defense by time frame, before, during and after attempted crime. Weapons, range, tactics, and more. Avail Sept 92

**AMMO FOREVER.    $12.95** Total self sufficiency for every gun you own. By Huber. Simplifies reloading for all guns. When the government shuts off supply, this book will keep your guns alive. Sept 92.

# These are your discount checks.

They work just the same as cash when used to purchase from Path Finder.
*DEALERS. We accept customer coupons from you as reverse keystone value
cash on our books.

---

FROM: _____
_____
_____          ____/____/____
                                      date

Pay to the order of: Path Finder Publications  // $2.50
          Two dollars and fifty cents _____

For: BOOKS                    _____

---

FROM: _____
_____
_____          ____/____/____
                                      date

Pay to the order of: Path Finder Publications  // $2.50
          Two dollars and fifty cents _____

For: BOOKS                    _____

---

FROM: _____
_____
_____          ____/____/____
                                      date

Pay to the order of: Path Finder Publications  // $5.00
          FIVE dollars -------------------------- _____

For: Hammocks/Compass         _____

---

Mail to:

## Path Finder Publications

1296 E. Gibson Rd., Suite 301  Woodland, Calif.   95776